CHEROKEE CLAIMS

FOR TRANSPORTATION AND SUBSISTENCE

Special File 154

Volume 1

Compiled by
Dawn C. Stricklin

HERITAGE BOOKS
2019

HERITAGE BOOKS
AN IMPRINT OF HERITAGE BOOKS, INC.

Books, CDs, and more—Worldwide

For our listing of thousands of titles see our website
at
www.HeritageBooks.com

Published 2019 by
HERITAGE BOOKS, INC.
Publishing Division
5810 Ruatan Street
Berwyn Heights, Md. 20740

International Standard Book Number
Paperbound: 978-1-58549-918-2

-Table of Contents-

Acknowledgements

I would like to thank Roberta M. Dorsey, MSW, LCSW for helping me with the editing of this book. As both a parent and a professional, I am proud to call her 'Mom'. To my husband and son, I thank them for their patience and encouragement. I would also like to thank my colleagues at the Association of Professional Genealogists at <www.apgen.org>. Living in a rural area, the APG mailing list enables me to network with other professionals without having to travel long distances. I have received both encouragement and advice from them, including my recent question about a bibliographical citation that is in this book. The National Archives also deserves my thanks. Their efforts in microfilming the documents that I transcribed in this book made it possible for me to work at home. Without these microfilmed records, I would have had to travel across the country to view them.

Introduction

The Special Files of the Office of Indian Affairs, 1807-1904, comprise eighty-five rolls of microfilm containing 303 Special Files. The transcribed and extracted documents in this volume are from *Special File 154, Cherokee Claims for Commutation of Transportation and Subsistence, treaty of 1835-36. 1845-55*. This book, the first of two volumes, was transcribed from National Archives micropublication M574, roll 32. These records can be viewed at the National Archives or can be purchased on microfilm. A descriptive pamphlet is also available for these records, but the index in the pamphlet is vague. In the descriptive pamphlet, only the names and subjects in the titles were indexed for the entire eighty-five rolls of microfilm, as well as a few documents that were deemed, "...of particular importance in the subject matter of files..."[1]. The lack of indexes creates a stumbling block for Cherokee researchers. However, the index to this book, along with its' second volume, should help to lessen that burden.

Most of the records in the Special Files series were compiled from incoming and outgoing correspondence and records of special commissions, notably the Third and Fourth Board of Cherokee Commissioners. In this volume, you will find the names of several commissioners who processed the Cherokee claims, including George C. Washington and John T. Mason (appointed June 1844, adjourned June 1845) from the third board, and Benjamin H. Brewster and Edward Harden (appointed July 1846, adjourned July 1847) from the fourth board[2]. For the most part however, correspondence pertains heavily to and from Richard C.S. Brown, agent for the Cherokee West of the Mississippi, and other United States government officials, along with numerous affidavits from individuals.

The documents in this book were created as a direct result of the 8th Article that was placed in the Treaty of New Echota. This article required that emigrating Cherokee were to be furnished with

---

[1] National Archives and Records Service, *Special Files of the Office of Indian Affairs,* Descriptive Pamphlet for M574 (Washington, D.C: National Archives and Records Service, 1971), 3.

[2] Edward E. Hill, *Guide to Records in the National Archives Relating to American Indians* (1981; reprint, Washington, D.C.: National Archives and Records Administration, 1981), 71.

one year's subsistence after their arrival in the Cherokee Nation West, and that the government would pay for the cost of their transportation. Article 8 also stipulated that certain Cherokee who were able to remove themselves would be allowed to do so and could substitute their one year's rations for a payment of $33.33, provided that a United States agent gave his approval. As a result, many Cherokee remained in the East long after the majority of the tribe emigrated to Indian Territory in 1838-1839. After arriving in the West, and in a few cases even before leaving the East, individuals had to prove their Cherokee citizenship to the United States government in order to receive their payment for transportation and subsistence. As a result, massive claims records were created.

The transcribed and extracted records in this book provide additional information for people researching Cherokee who are listed on the 1835 Census, or Henderson Roll. However, several names of Cherokee citizens who are not on that census have been revealed in these records. Dr. Lathel F. Duffield wrote an article citing omissions in the Henderson Roll, stating that it "*...should not be the sole document used when attempting to identify the Cherokee of that era...*"[3] (emphasis added). The absence of an individual's name on that census does not mean that they were not Cherokee. Instead, other records should be searched for evidence of Cherokee ancestry.

In compiling this publication, my goals were to make this data, often overlooked by many researchers, available to everyone in printed form and to create an index so that the microfilmed records could be easily accessed. I urge everyone to use this book as a reference for locating the original record.

Census rolls are an important part of Cherokee genealogical and historical research. However, there are other records that can provide just as good, if not better, evidence of Cherokee ancestry. These records provide a glimpse into the individual lives of people before, during, and after their removal to Indian Territory. This volume testifies to the wide range of records that are available for people interested in Cherokee history and genealogy, and it has been

---

[3] Lathel F. Duffield. "Questionable Honor: An Analysis of the 1835 Cherokee Census ("Henderson Roll")," *National Genealogical Society Quarterly* 90 (September 2002): 235.

my pleasure to bring to you this small portion of those massive documents.

How to Use this Book

This book can be a highly effective research tool if readers know how to approach it. First of all, there is no substitute for an original record. Once you have located the person you are seeking in this volume, use the citation above it and procure a photocopy of the original. Second, the documents in this volume can lead you to other areas of research. This collection of transcriptions and extracts are by no means the final word on Cherokee documents. There are massive amounts of records concerning the Cherokee Indians. After locating the original, continue to search for primary documents for your ancestor. At the back of the book is a bibliography and a suggested reading list. The publications provided in these two sections will increase your knowledge of the availability of other Cherokee documents and how to access them.

At the end of this volume are three appendixes. Appendix A provides a short description of the linguistic problems that researchers will encounter in this volume, and generally in all other areas of Cherokee research. Appendix B references the various marks and notations that were placed in the transcriptions and extracts, and gives an explanation of each, and Appendix C explains how to read the citations that are listed with each set of documents. Please take a few moments to read through the Appendixes. The more familiar you are with the book's format, the easier it will be to read and understand the records contained in it.

Cherokee Claims for Commutation of Transportation and Subsistence, Treaty of 1835-36. 1845-55. Special File 154, frame 3, Special Files of the Office of Indian Affairs; National Archives micropublication M574, roll 32.

[*page begins*]

"Particulars of the 74- Claims.-
Cherokees.
Nov. 11. 1845

SPECIAL FILE No 154"
[*end of page*]

Cherokee Claims for Commutation of Transportation and Subsistence, Treaty of 1835-36. 1845-55. Special File 154, frame 4, Special Files of the Office of Indian Affairs; National Archives micropublication M574, roll 32.
[*Note: this document has been extracted, not transcribed. The information that has not been included in this extract are certificate date, number in family, and amount paid. You can acquire this information by viewing the microfilmed copy.*]

"...List- of Cherokee Claimants- for transportation- & Subsistence...

...Names...	...Residence...
David Hilderbrand	
John Hilderbrand	
Mary Hilderbrand	
Rance Bird Harris	
Margarett Catron	
Nancy Levit	
Sarah Nicholson	
(for her husband- J.R. Nicholson)	
Peggy Contagu	oostenula
Eliza Woolf- Turtle	old nation

Betsy Covel- Turtle	do
Tee-nah, na-lah	
Jane Cookson (husband Joseph Cookson)	
Henry Morton	old cherokee nation- Forsyth county, G[a]
Elizabeth Thompson	old nation
Joel J. Morton	" "
Elizabeth Alan	Conesaugee river old nation
Sally or Sarah	Coosa- Floyd County, G[a]
T. Jefferson Pack	Wills Valley
Arch M[c]Daniel	Cass Co. G[a]
Daniel Cade	old nation
Polly Cade	" " ..."

Particulars for the 74 Cherokee Claims for Commutation of Transportation and Subsistence, Treaty of 1835-36. 1845-55. Special File 154, frame 5, Special Files of the Office of Indian Affairs; National Archives micropublication M574, roll 32.

[*page begins*]
[*Note: There are two frames numbered '5'. This is the first of the set.*]

"Particulars of the 74- claims.-
Cherokees.
Nov. 11.1845.

SPECIAL FILE No 154"
[*end of page*]
[*end of document*]

Cherokee Claims for Commutation of Transportation and Subsistence, Treaty of 1835-36. 1845-55. Special File 154, frame 5, Special Files of the Office of Indian Affairs; National Archives micropublication M574, roll 32.

[*page begins*]
[*Note: There are two frames numbered '5'. This is the second of the set.*]

"A1909

Emign [*sic*] Cherokee
Second Auditor,
Nov. 10, 1845.

In reference to Cherokee commuted transportation & subsistence claims- List ~~of~~ (1283) of those referred to that office accompanying with result of examination annuled [*sic*] in each case- Papers referred returned- "A general abstract of payments for commuted transportation and Subsistence, under cherokee treaty of 1835" also accompanying- makes certain requests- &c

Papers left by Butler B2531 returned to him, Aug. 1846.

Rec^{d} 11. Nov. 1845."
[*end of page*]
[*end of document*]

Letter from Jno. M. McCalla to William Medill. Cherokee Claims for Commutation of Transportation and Subsistence, Treaty of 1835-36. 1845-55. Special File 154, frames 6-8, Special Files of the Office of Indian Affairs; National Archives micropublication M574, roll 32.

[*page begins*]
[*first page*]

"Treasury Department
Second Auditor's Office
Novem: 10th 1845.

Sir,

An examination has been made of the Claims of Sundry Cherokees for balances alledged [*sic*] to be due them by the government, on account of commuted Transportation and Subsistence, under the treaty of the 29th Decem^{r} 1835:- as referred to this Office, by the Comm^{r} of Indian Affairs- on the 19th – 21st - & 27th August- and 17th Septem^{r}- last: and I send herewith a List- (Nos: 1, 2, 3) of the Claims referred to this office, as above mentioned by the Comm. Of Indian Affairs, with the result of the Examination annexed to each case.

Tho much care has been employed in order to obtain a correct result, as to each claim- difficulties have been met with, in relation to a number of them, involving some uncertainty as to their actual and true position. Such cases are distinguished on the list, by leaving the amount in the column aggregate balances- blank. Having some doubts in regard to the claims which are not here reports as fully paid off- I respectfully request that Such administrative action may be had in the Indian bureau, previous to a final decision by the accounting Officers, as may conduce to a correct issue.

The certificates, copies, and affidavits on which the"
[*end of page*]

[*second page*]
"several claims are based, with the Letters of Gov: Butler and the letters of the Commissioner of Indian Affairs- which accompanied their reference to this office, are returned, here with, as requested: and also the Muster Rolls, as furnished by Mr Barling.- Capt: Stephenson's Clerk.

For the purpose of Settling with correctness and dispatch, claims of this description for the future- I have caused a careful Examination to be made, of all disbursements for transportation and Subsistence of the Cherokees- by Agents, East and West of the Mississippi,- and a full Abstract of all payments made by way of commutation, under the treaty of 1835. When any claim of this class shall be presented hereafter, instead of going through the tedious process of Searching the files of the numerous Settlements of the disbursing Agents, who have received and paid out their funds- it will only be necessary to look over this Abstract, and ascertain the payments, if any, which may have been made, and the balance remaining due may be promptly determined.

As it is proposed to decide such claims as may arise here after, by a reference to this Abstract, so far, at last, as related to the question of payments here tofore [*sic*] made, I respectfully request, that it may be critically Examined in the Office of Indian Affairs, and if found defective, that such remarks be made, as may render it competent to the object in view.

With the foregoing observations- the List of claims, and the general Abstract for future use, in the Settlement of"
[*end of page*]

[*third page*]
"of [*sic*] similar claims are respectfully transmitted herewith- with the request, that when they have received the official action of the Commissioner of Indian Affairs, they may be returned to this Office with the result of said official action, in writing.

Most respectfully Your Ob: Ser:-
Jn° M. McCalla-
[*his signature*]

2^d Auditor.

William Medill Esquire
Comm^r In: Affs:"
[*end of page*]
[*end of document*]

George Fields and John Fields Claims, Cherokee Claims for Commutation of Transportation and Subsistence, Treaty of 1835-36. 1845-55, Special File 154, frames 9-11, Special Files of the Office of Indian Affairs; National Archives micropublication M574, roll 32.

[*first page*]

"A1909 B.2510
Emgn Cherokee

P.M. Butler, Ch. Agt.
Cherokee Agency, 30 June '45

Encloses Cherokee Subsistence certificate with affidavits in cases when the certificates have been lost.- certificates of John & Geo. Fields returned-

Request that examination be made and payments ordered at an early day, the claimants being poor &c

Red[d] 7th Augt. 1845
Ans[d.] 19 Aug[t.]- See letters of 19 Aug[t] to 2[d]. Auditor also.-
over

Respectfully referred, to the 2 auditor- To be considered in view of the certificates for commutation of Subs. of Geo & Jno Fields here tofore Sent to his office

Office Ind: Affairs
Aug[t] 22. 1845

[*Note: the writing below was faint and very hard to read. In addition. there is line across part of the writing, apparently when the document was microfilmed, that increases the illegibility of the writing. Please refer to original document.*]

Certificates of Nancy Fields, Ira Goddard Jno R Blythe- examined & allowed. [*S*]ee letter to S.M. Ruth[*er*]f[*or*]d Ap[l] 16[*?*] 1849[*?*] Geo[*?*] Fields case suspended"
[*end of page*]

[*second page*]

"Cherokee Agency
30th June 1845

Sir,

I herewith enclose you all the certificates of Subsistence that I have been enabled to collect, together with affidavits, in cases where the certificats [*sic*] have been lost.

I return again for further examination the certificates of George and John Fields, the former you will discover, has made an affidavit that he has never been paid any thing for Subsistence; he is an old and respectable man, and I think entitled to respect and confidence. There being two other persons by the name of George Fields, who emigrated and Subsisted themselves, and have been paid, it is probable that the payment you allude to in your letter of the [*smudged date*] April last was made to one of those persons, and not to the present claimant. By a comparison of the certificates (the number in family showing the amount to be paid) with the vouchers, that fact can be ascertained. John Fields is a similar case.

I have respectfully to request, that the examinations be made, and payments ordered at as early a day as profitable, the claimants being poor and clamorous.-"

[*end of page*]

[*third page*]

"I have the honor to be very
Respectfuly [*sic*] Your ob^{t}. Servt.
P.M. Butler [*his signature*]
Ch. Agent

T Hartley Crawford Esqr
Comm^{r} Ind. Affrs.
Washington city"

[*end of page*]

[*end of document*]

Letter from T. Hartley Crawford to Jno. M. McCalla, Transportation and Subsistence, Referred to the 2d Aud. Off 29 Aug- 1845.-, Cherokee Claims for Commutation of Transportation and Subsistence, Treaty of 1835-36. 1845-55. Special File 154, frames 12-13, Special Files of the Office of Indian Affairs; National Archives micropublication M574, roll 32.

[*first page*]

"Office Indn Affairs
Aug. 27. 1845
A1909
T.H. Crawford
Recd. Aug. 27. 1845
Ansd.

Mr J.W. Brown"
[*end of page*]

[*second page*]

"War Department
Office Indian Affairs
August 27. 1845

Sir,

I have the honor to enclose herewith a list of the names of certain Cherokee emigrants who claim the commutation allowance for transportation & Subsistence under the treaty of 1835, with the papers offered by them in Support of their claims. I will thank you to cause the rolls of Cherokee Emigrants filed in your office, and the accounts of the disbursing officers who made payments to Cherokee emigrants on account of transportation and Subsistence, to be examined to ascertain whether the names of these Cherokees are on the rolls, and whether any money, and if any, how much, is due to the claimants respectively-

Be so obliging as to communicate to me the result of the examination, and at the Same time return the papers for the further action of this office.

very respectfully
yr. ob[t] Serv[t]
T. Hartley Crawford.
[*his signature*]

Gen[l] Jno. M M[c]Calla
2[d] Auditor &c"
[*end of page*]
[*end of document*]

List of Cherokee Claimants, Transportation and Subsistence, Referred to the 2[d] Aud. Off. 29 Aug- 1845. Cherokee Claims for Commutation of Transportation and Subsistence, Treaty of 1835-36. 1845-55. Special File 154, frames 14-15, Special Files of the Office of Indian Affairs; National Archives micropublication M574, roll 32.

[*first page*]

"A1909
List of Cherokee Claimants
Transportation and Subsistence-
referred to the 2[d] aud[s] off 29. Aug- 1845-"
[*end of page*]

[*second page*]

"List of certain Cherokee Emigrants who claim commutation for transportation and Subsistence under the treaty of 1835- forwarded to the office of Indian Affairs by Gov[r] Butler under different dates- and now transmitted to the Second Auditor for examination and to be returned to the office of Indian Affairs for further action

Moses Hilderbrand
David Hilderbrand allowed See letter to Rutherford 16 Apl '49
John Hilderbrand
Elizabeth Thompson
Henry Morton allowed see letter to Rutherford 16 Apl '49

Elizabeth Ware
Joel J. Morton Suspended see letter 16 Apl '49
Sarah Nicholson
Peggy Contagu
Polly Cade
Dan[l] Cade
Arch M[c]Daniel
T Jefferson Pack
Sally or Sarah (wife of Itte cun-na hee) allowed & Paid
Margaret Catrone See letter Sup Rutherford 26 Apl '48
Jane Cookson (wife of Jos: Cookson do-do
Reese Mitchell do-do
Tee-nah-na-lah
Rance Bird Harris Dis allowed see letter 18 March '48
Eliza Wolf (formerly Eliza Turtle) Suspended see }
Betsy Covel (formerly Betsy Turtle) letter 16 April 49 }
Nancy Levit Allowed see letter 16 April '49

Office Ind. Affairs
August 24. 1845"

[*end of page*]
[*end of document*]

Letter from T. Hartley Crawford, Cherokee Claims for Commutation of Transportation and Subsistence, Treaty of 1835-36. 1845-55. Special File 154, frame 16-18, Special Files of the Office of Indian Affairs; National Archives micropublication M574, roll 32.

[*first page*]

"Office Ind[n] Affrs.
Aug. 19. 1845
A1909
T. Hartley Crawford
Rec[d] Aug. 20. 1845

Ans[d]
Mr J.W. Brown"
[*end of page*]

[*second page*]

"War Department
Office of Indian Affairs
August 19. 1845

Sir

Under date of 30th June ult., Gov[r.] Butler, Cherokee Agent, forwarded to this office the Several papers herein enclosed, viz: Eleven certificates, and four copies of Similar ones, the originals being retained by Indians; these certificates, as you will perceive, were given to Cherokee emigrants by Gen[l] N. Smith, late Sup[t] of Cherokee Emigration, and State that the holders having commuted their transportation, were permitted to emigrate themselves to their new Country west, where they would be entitled on their arrival, to receive one year's Subsistence, or in lieu thereof, $33 33/100. The holders of these certificates now claim, Some of them the whole, others in part, (as will appear from the papers) of the Sum allowed in lieu of Subsistence.

Gov[r.] Butler forwarded at the Same time, the affidavits of Seven other emigrants stating that they also received certificates but which are no longer in their possession for reasons stated by them. One or two of these claim for transportation as well as Subsistence

All"
[*end of page*]

[*third page*]

All the certificates, copies. and affidavits above mentioned

are respectfully referred to your office that and [*e*]xamination therein may be made to ascertain whether or not any money is due to these emigrant Cherokees, and if any, how much to each claimant.

You will receive herewith the claim of George Baldrige for like Subsistence, forwarded by Gov[r] B, as above mentioned, Supported by affidavit, wherein, however, it is not stated. as in the other cases, that he had received a certificate, this claim also is respectfully referred to your office for examination.

After the examination is had in your office, I will thank you to return the papers with ~~your report~~ the result of your examination [*inserted*] to this office for its further action in the premises

Very respectfully
Yr obt Sert
T. Hartley Crawford
[*his signature*]

Genl J.M. McCalla
2d Auditor &c
[*end of page*]
[*end of document*]

Ross B. Daniel, Cherokee Claims for Commutation of Transportation and Subsistence, Treaty of 1835-36. 1845-55. Special File 154, frames 19-21, Special Files of the Office of Indian Affairs; National Archives micropublication M574, roll 32.

[*first page*]
"A1909

B2510
Ross B. Daniel

4 in family-
2 increase= 6
emigrated in 1838

name on Roll No 4- for 4 persons in family"
[*end of page*]

[*second page*]

"Personally appeared before me (P.M Butler Cherokee Agent) Robt B. Daniel (who is clerk of the Supreme Court) & makes oath that in the ~~Spring~~ Fall of 1837- he commuted his

Rations for four in family- & held a certificate from Nat. Smith which certificate was paid in full, first one half- by Lt. Van Horn & the other by Capt. Stevenson.

That he resided in Long Swamp Georgia- (now Cherokee County- now resided in Delaware District Cherokee Nation- that he did not Emigrate till the Spring of 1838 that then were two Souls- more in family- at the time of removal that at the time of commuting; one by an increase of his family (& by the confinement of his wife was the cause of detention)- the other a slave about 5 years of age- given to his wife Ann- by her mother- he now prays the amount of $66.66 2/3 Subsistence & & [*sic*] $40- for transportation, he semitted [*sic*] to the Agent for his use

In all ______________________ $106.66 2/3

Sworn to & Subscribed
before me this 26 June   Robt. B. Daniel [*his signature*]
1845 P.M. Butler Ch agt.

Also appeared Mrs Susanna Taylor"
[*end of page*]

[*third page*]

"& testifies to the facts de tailed [*sic*] mother by R. B. Daniel; & in addition that the Slave ~~was~~ (David) was given to her Daughter- with out the knowledge at the time of commuting by R.B Daniel further that this Slave was not included in the tras portation [*sic*] or Subsis tence [*sic*] or any other person-

her
Sworn to before me   Susanna X Taylor
this day 26 June 1843   mark

P.M. Butler [*his signature*]
Ch Agent"

[*end of page*]
[*end of document*]

Cherokee Claims for Commutation of Transportation and Subsistence, Treaty of 1835-36. 1845-55. Special File 154, frame 22-24, Special Files of the Office of Indian Affairs; National Archives micropublication M574, roll 32.

[*first page*]
[*Note: on this frame there is an addition of numbers. This information has not been transcribed.*]

"B2531
A1909

[*below in upside down writing*]
M. Duvall Esqr PM
Fort Gibson"
[*end of page*]

[*second page*]

[*Note: on this frame there is an addition of numbers. This information has not been transcribed. This frame is an exact copy of frame 22, except that the paper was microfilmed at a different angle.*]
[*end of page*]

[*third page*]

Sulphur Springs C. Cty
11th March 1845

Sir

Agreeably to the request of Go^v Butler I herewith transmit to you the Original muster Rolls of Cherokees who have pay due them for Subsistence.

I would say to you that persons bringing in certificates, that you will find them marked paid on these Rolls as also for the Certificates.

Please take care of the Rolls

Resp[y] Yours
Aaron Barling [*his signature*]

M. Duvall Esq[r]}
F[t] Gibson }"
[*end of page*]
[*end of document*]

Cherokee Claims for Commutation of Transportation and Subsistence, Treaty of 1835-36. 1845-55. Special File 154, frame 25, Special Files of the Office of Indian Affairs; National Archives micropublication M574, roll 32.

[*page begins*]

"No. 1-
SPECIAL FILE No 154"
[*end of page*]
[*end of document*]

Cherokee Claims for Commutation of Transportation and Subsistence, Treaty of 1835-36. 1845-55. Special File 154, frame 26, Special Files of the Office of Indian Affairs; National Archives micropublication M574, roll 32.

[*page begins*]

"A1909"
[*end of page*]
[*end of document*]

Certificate Given to Cherokee Emigrants Who Were Permitted to Remove Themselves, Cherokee Claims for Commutation of Transportation and Subsistence, Treaty of 1835-36. 1845-55. Special File 154, frame 27, Special Files of the Office of Indian Affairs; National Archives micropublication M574, roll 32.

[*page begins*]
"Certificates given to Cherokee Emigrants by Genl N. Smith
Showing they were permit[1] to remove themselves &c

Viz:	Richd Fields	Paid
	S.W. Bell	Filed-
	Ira Goddard	Paid
	David M. Harlin	Filed
	Nelly Martin	Filed
	Nancy Fields	Paid
	John R Blythe	Paid
	John Fields	Filed
	Geo Fields	sent back
	John Kell	
	John Tedwell	

Forwarded by Govr Butler 30 June 1845.
These are all found on the rolls- in the Ind office-"
[*end of page*]
[*end of document*]

[1] The rest of the letters for this word was missing, either due to a crease in the paper or there was a small piece of paper covering this portion.

Certificate Given to Cherokee Emigrants Who Were Permitted to Remove Themselves, Cherokee Claims for Commutation of Transportation and Subsistence, Treaty of 1835-36. 1845-55. Special File 154, frame 28, Special Files of the Office of Indian Affairs; National Archives micropublication M574, roll 32.

[*page begins*]

"No. 2

Copies of certificates given by Genl N Smith to Cherokee Emigrants Showing they were permitted to remove themselves west &c. viz:

~~Geo Baldrige~~
Alexander Raper
Felix Arthur
David Kell
A. Scudder
~~Ty[?] Ky[?]~~

A1909

These names are found on the rolls in the Ind. Office"
[*end of page*]
[*end of document*]

Arch McDaniel Claim for Transportation and Subsistence, Cherokee Claims for Commutation of Transportation and Subsistence, Treaty of 1835-36. 1845-55. Special File 154, frame 29-32, Special Files of the Office of Indian Affairs; National Archives micropublication M574, roll 32.

[*first page*]

"20.
Arch McDaniel
B2454 A1909
" 448

No. 16"
[*end of page*]

[*second page*]

"The United States
To Arch McDaniel

To transportation and subsistence due him by the United States as follows-

Transportation from Cass Co Geo^{a} in the year 1837, under the}
Treaty of 1835.- } 20.00

To Subsistence one year for himself after his arrival west pr. }
Treaty 1835. } 33.33

<u>$53.33</u>

Personally appeared before me P.M. Butler Cherokee agent, Arch McDaniel, (a cherokee) who being duly sworn deposes as follows- that he emigrated to the Cherokee Nation West under the Treaty of 1835- in the spring of 1837 that he did not enroll in the Nation East- and that he never has received either transportation or subsistence money and[*?*] rations in any manner- neither commutation or in kind and that the sum of Fifty-three dollars 23/100- is just due him now for the same- never having received payment for the same.-"
[*end of page*]

[*third page*]

"That he arrived in the Nation West, about the 1st May 1837.- That he has no subsistence or transportation certificate nor ever has.- ~~and~~

Arch X McDaniel
[*his mark*]

Before me this day 12 Apl 1845
<u>P.M. Butler</u>
[*his signature*]
Cherokee Agent

Sam[l] Mayes- citizen of cherokee nation by marriage- being duly sworn before me P.M. Butler, cherokee agent- says- that he is well acquainted with the claimant Arch M[c]Daniel- knows that he did emigrate as stated in 1837- that he lived with deponent some time before his removal; - and that he started in company with him- and travelled [*sic*] together as far as Nashville- when they seperated [*sic*];- that on deponents arrival west about 10th of May1837: he found said Arch M[c]Daniel already here in this country- that he M[c]Daniel again came to live with him- and did stay some month or two- and further"
[*end of page*]

[*fourth page*]

"to the best of his deponents knowledge and belief the amount charged for his transportation & subsistence is still due.-

Samuel Mayes
[*his signature*]

Before me this day 12 Ap[l] 1845
P.M. Butler
[*his signature*]"
Ch. Agent"
[*end of page*]
[*end of document*]

Rance Bird Harris Emigration, Cherokee Claims for Commutation of Transportation and Subsistence, Treaty of 1835-36. 1845-55. Special File 154, frame 33-36, Special Files of the Office of Indian Affairs; National Archives micropublication M574, roll 32.

[*first page*]

"4.
A1909
B2442
Rance Bird Harris

N$^{o.}$ 23.

[*in faint handwriting below. Please reference original*]
See Joel Crittendens acc^{t}- 2^{d} qr 1838- where it will probably appear that part at least of this has been paid. off[?] Ind affairs"
[*end of page*]

[*second page*]

"Cherokee Agency East
April 7, 1838

Rance Bird Harris is permitted to remove himself and Family to the Country assigned the Cherokees West of the Mississippi having commuted the Transportation and Years Subsistence. His Family consist[*s*] of Self, Wife, one Son under Ten, two Male and two Female Slaves.

He will report to the Agent of the Cherokees on his arrival in the Cherokee Country West.

For
Genl Nathl Smith [*his signature*]
Supt^{t} Ch Rem^{l}
J.N. Hetzel [*his signature*]"

[*end of page*]

[*third page*]

"United States To
Ranse Bird Harris

To transportation for five Slaves $20-	100 00
" Subsistance [*sic*] for the Same $33.33 1/3)5	166 2/3

We do hereby certify that R Bird Harris emigrated to this country in the year 1843 and brought with him the above number of Slaves
March 29th 1845

J.B. Collins [*his signature*]
Joseph Rogers [*his signature*]

Personally appeared before me R.B. Harris- & makes oath in due form of Law that the above account- is just & true, & that he has never received any part there of- R B Harris [*his signature*]

P.M. Butler [*his signature*]
Cherokee Agent
Also the names of J.B. Collins & Jo^{s} Rogers
P.M.B. Ch. Agt. was identified before me"
[*end of page*]

[*fourth page*]

"Commissioner's office-
March 29. 1845- J.B. Collins and R. B. Harris appeared before me and were fully identified by satisfactory evidence to be the proper persons named in the foregoing instrument
John T. Mason [*his signature*]"
[*end of page*]
[*end of document*]

Claim of Eliza Wolf and Betsey Covel, Cherokee Claims for Commutation of Transportation and Subsistence, Treaty of 1835-36. 1845-55. Special File 154, frame 37, Special Files of the Office of Indian Affairs; National Archives micropublication M574, roll 32.

[*Note: this frame is identical to frame 39, with the exception that frame 39 was microfilmed at a different angle*]

Claim of Eliza Wolf and Betsey Covel, Cherokee Claims for Commutation of Transportation and Subsistence, Treaty of 1835-36. 1845-55. Special File 154, frame 38, Special Files of the Office of Indian Affairs; National Archives micropublication M574, roll 32.

[*page begins*]

"The Unted States To
EllizaWolf- and
1845.- To. Betsy Covel.}Dr.

Subsistence- Eliza and Betsy Turtle (Cherokees) emigrees from the "Old Nation" to the "Cherokee Nation West" at 33 1/3 per head-
$66.66

Credit the amount by $34.40
leaving a balance of $32.26 -

[*illegible*]

Subsistence Balance	$-32.26
Transportation- $20.00 per head.	40.00
	$72.26

Cherokee Nation Agency} April 3rd 1845

Before me this day personally appeared Eliza Wolf,- formerly Eliza Turtle (a cherokee) and deposeth, that Her self the deponent (-and her Sister Betsy, now Betsy Covel [*inserted*], emigrated to this country in the Family of Eleazer Butler, a "missionary" of the "American Board of Commissioners for Foreign Missions"- in the year A.D. 1839- that she believes the above account to be correct and true, that the amount credited $34.40, is all that has been paid upon the amount, and that they have never received from any source, any pay or renumeration- the[?] than that above credited.

Eliza Wolf [*her signature*]
3 Apl 1845

Before me
P.M. Butler Ch Agt.
[*his signature*]"
[*end of page*]
[*end of document*]

Claim of Eliza Wolf and Betsey Covel, Cherokee Claims for Commutation of Transportation and Subsistence, Treaty of 1835-36. 1845-55. Special File 154, frame 39, Special Files of the Office of Indian Affairs; National Archives micropublication M574, roll 32.

[*page begins*]
[*Note: there appears to be some writing on this document that is very faint and hard to read. That writing has not been included in this transcription. Please reference original document.*]

"9. 10. D268 D.1030
R.304
Claim of Eliza Wolf and Betsey Wolf
A1909

Suspended
I would suggest the allowance of this claim

N° 24 & 25

Additional
Testimony

X
This claim was ret[*urn*]ed to this office 25th June 1846.

[*illegible*] Du Val, attorney is hereby authorized to receive Ten per cent upon the amount collected on their claim, and the disbursing agent is requested to pay the same-
April 3rd 1845-

Eliza Wolfe
[*her signature*]"

[*end of page*]
[*end of document*]

Additional Affidavit of Eliza J. Wolf, May 27, 1848, Cherokee Claims for Commutation of Transportation and Subsistence, Treaty of 1835-36. 1845-55. Special File 154, frame 40-41, Special Files of the Office of Indian Affairs; National Archives micropublication M574, roll 32.

[*first page*]

"additional affadavit [*sic*] of Eliza J. Wolf.
May 27[d] 1848."
[*end of page*]

[*second page*]

"Cherokee Nation West
Cherokee Agency

Now on this day before me R.C.S. Brown . Cherokee Agent, personally came Eliza Wolf , a Cherokee Woman, who after being duly Sworn States that she and Betsy Covel Each of whom are named in her affadavit [*sic*] here before me made before Gov[r] Butler, when agent for the Cherokee Nation, Sworn to on the 3rd day of April 1845. an [*sic*] both Cherokee, Each of whom have here to fore resided for many years in the Cherokee Nation East, were recognized there by the authorities, and Entitled to the usual priviliges of other Cherokees

Affiant States that She and Betsy Covel were Sisters and that in May 1838, their Father Little Turtle a Cherokee died and their Mother haveing [*sic*] been dead for Several years, their father Requested that his Children, generally, should be under the Charge and control. of John Eleazer Butler a missionary of the American Board of Commissioners, for foreign Missions ," Affiant further States, that She, and her Sister, Betsy Covel, left the old Cherokee Nation East, in the month of April 1839, in company with Doctor Eleazer Butler, Missionary as aforesaid, and his family for the Cherokee Nation West, and arrived in Western, Cherokee nation Some time in the month of June, same year, and affiant, and Said Betsy Covel, have both resided in the Western Cherokee Nation

ever Since, and are permanently settled, and recognized by the Cherokee Authorities, Entitled to usual privileges of other Cherokees, affiant States neither She, nor her, Sister, never were enrolled to the Best of her knowledge in any family or company for Emigration, that She and her Sister Removed from the Eastern, to the, Western Cherokee Nation and Subsisted themselves during such removal, and for Twelve Months then after upon their own Exclusive means, affiant further States, that she nor her sister, never were before removed at the Expense of the United States, nor the Cherokee People, only any one who was paid therefor, and that neither she nor her sister, ever have at any time, received from the United States, any Commutation, of Transportation and Subsistence, Either in Money or in kind, Save the Thirty four dollars and forty cents, as specified in her affadavit [*sic*], made before Gov[r] Butler, and now on file, which Said amount was handed to affiant, and her sister, by Doc[r] Eliazer Butler, further the deponant saith not
Sworn to and Subscribed before me
This 27th day of May 1848------ Elisa T. Wolf
[*her signature*]

RCS Brown. Cherokee Agent"
[*end of page*]
[*end of document*]

George Fields Claim, Cherokee Claims for Commutation of Transportation and Subsistence, Treaty of 1835-36. 1845-55. Special File 154, frames 42-43, Special Files of the Office of Indian Affairs; National Archives micropublication M574, roll 32.

[*first page*]
[*Note: there appears to be some writing on this document that is very faint and hard to read. That writing has not been included in this transcription. Please reference original document.*]

"23.
A1909 + R305
B[2]510- B[?]729

Geo Fields

N°. 32

X"
[*end of page*]

[*second page*]

"Cherokee Agency East
Febry 15th, 1838

George Fields, a Cherokee from Grasshopper creek is permitted to remove himself and Family, consisting of Eight persons, viz self, wife, one son under the [*age of*] Ten, Two daughters under, ten and Three over ten years of age, to the country assigned the Cherokee West of the Mississippi, having commuted the transportation. He will report to the agent of the Cherokees on his arrival in the Cherokee country West (signed) Nat Smith

[*his signature*]
Supt Cher removals

A true copy from the original left with me this day to be for warded to Washington City to be compared verified & returned for payment

P.M. Butler
[*his signature*]
Ch. Agent

Cherokee Agency
1 March 1845

Personally appeared before me, George Fields, who being sworn, says, that he is the owner, and has in possession a certificate, of which the above is a copy, and that he has never received any pay from the U.S government for subsistence to which said certificate entitles him.

George Fields
[*his signature*]
Grass hopper Creek

Sworn to & Subscribed before me this 30 June 1845

P.M. Butler
[*his signature*]
Ch. Agt."

[*end of page*]
[*end of document*]

Nelly Martin Permission to Remove Family, Cherokee Claims for Commutation of Transportation and Subsistence, Treaty of 1835-36. 1845-55. Special File 154, frames 44-45, Special Files of the Office of Indian Affairs; National Archives micropublication M574, roll 32.

[*first page*]

"29.
Nelly Martin
X

Nelly Martin
B. 2510
A1909"
[*end of page*]

[*second page*]

"Cherokee Agency
19th Nov. 1838

Nelly Martin the [*illegible*] and head of a Cherokee family, is permitted to remove herself & family, consisting of four sons, & an daughter over Ten & an orphan girl under Ten years of age to the Country assigned the Cherokees West of the mississippi [*sic*]

She having been paid one hundred & Sixty dollars for their transportat[*ion*]

She will report to the Agent of the Cherokees on her arrival

West.

Nat Smith
[*his signature*]
Sup[t]. Ch. Em.

Paid ¼ 22nd Ap[l] 1839"
[*end of page*]
[*end of document*]

David M. Harlin Permission to Remove Family, Cherokee Claims for Commutation of Transportation and Subsistence, Treaty of 1835-36. 1845-55. Special File 154, frames 46-47, Special Files of the Office of Indian Affairs; National Archives micropublication M574, roll 32.

[*first page*]

"30.

X

B. 2510
A1909
D.M Harlin

paid."
[*end of page*]

[*second page*]

"Cherokee Agency East
May 14, 1838

David M. Harlin having commuted the Transportation is permitted to remove himself, wife, Two Sons, under Ten years of age, and one daughter, under Ten, to the Country assigned the Cherokees west of the Mississippi.

He will report to the Agent of the Cherokees on his arrival

in the Cherokee Country West.

Nat Smith
[*his signature*]
Sup[t]. Ch. Removal

P 14 25th July
C.V."
[*end of page*]
[*end of document*]

Samuel W. Bell Permission to Remove Family, Cherokee Claims for Commutation of Transportation and Subsistence, Treaty of 1835-36. 1845-55. Special File 154, frames 48-49, Special Files of the Office of Indian Affairs; National Archives micropublication M574, roll 32.

[*first page*]
[*Note: there are some numbers and also what appears to be an addition of numbers located at the bottom of the page in very faint handwriting. This information has not been transcribed. See original for reference.*]

"32.

A1909

S W Bell

Trans & Subs
all paid

[*below at the bottom of the page written upside down*]
B. 2510"
[*end of page*]

[*second page*]

"Cherokee Agency East
November 7, 1838

Sam[l] W. Bell, a Cherokee, having commuted the transportation is permitted to remove himself and male Slave to the Country assigned the Cherokees west of the Mississippi.

He will report tot he Agent of the Cherokees on his arrival in the Cherokee Country West.

Nat Smith
[*his signature*]
Sup[t]. Ch. Em.

Pd ½ 11 Ma[*r*]ch 1839
P. M K"
[*end of page*]
[*end of document*]

William Dameron Claim, Cherokee Claims for Commutation of Transportation and Subsistence, Treaty of 1835-36. 1845-55. Special File 154, frames 50-52, Special Files of the Office of Indian Affairs; National Archives micropublication M574, roll 32.

[*first page*]

"39. N. 8 A1909
W[m] Dameron
N[o.] 46.

immigrated in 1838

[*in faint handwriting below*]
name not found on Roll of those who were permitted to remove themselves
B2510

[*written vertically on the left side of the paper*]
A true copy from the original left with [*written over 'by me'*] this day & to be forwarded to the com: of Ind. Affairs- at washington [*sic*] for information & action.-

P.M. Butler [*his signature*]
Ch: Agt.

Fort Gibson
Ch: Nation
6th Feb. 1845"
[*end of page*]

[*second page*]

"cherokee Nation}
Ft. Gibson }

Personally appeared before me P.M. Butler Cherokee agent, Samuel Mayes who being duly sworn, makes oath. That he is personally knowing [*sic*] to William Dameron (who has a cherokee family) emigrating and subsisting himself and family on their removal from the Cherokee Nation East, under the Treaty of 1835 in the Spring 1838 he obtained a certificate from Genl. Nat Smith who was then emigrating agent certifying that he Wm Dameron did emigrate and Subsist himself as provided for- which certificate he filed with Capt. Stevenson then disbursing agent.

Samuel Mayes
[*his signature*]

Sworn to & subscribed before me this 9th May 1842.
P.M Butler
Cherokee agent

Cherokee Nation }
Going Snake District}

Personaly [*sic*] appeared before me John T. Adair one of the associate Judges of the Supreme Court, Samuel Mayes and makes oath in due form Saith that the Certificate of Genl. Nat Smith as sworn to above before P.M. Butler U.S.agent given to Wm Dameron for emigrating and Subsisting himself specifies three in family, and that he has reasons to believe and does believe that the Said Wm Dameron has never received any compensation for the Same from the united States or any other Source whatever.

Samuel Mayes
[*his signature*]

Sworn to and Subscribed before me this 1st Feby. 1845
John T. Adair
[*his signature*]
Asst. Judge Spr. Court."

[*end of page*]

[*third page*]

"Cherokee Nation }
Going Snake District}

Pe[*r*]sonally appeared before me John T. Adair associate Judge of the Supreme Court Wm Dameron makes oath in due form Saith that he emigrated from the Cherokee Nation East to the Cherokee west in the Spring of 1837. that he removed himself and family at his own expense and never has received from the united States or any of the agents or from any other Source whatsoever any com Pensation [*sic*] for the Same or for any part thereof.

Wm Dameron
[*his signature*]

Sworn to and Subscribed before me this 1st day of Feby. 1845.
John T. Adair
Asst. Judge. Spr. C[*o*]urt.

A true copy from the original left with me this day & to be forwarded to the com: of Ind: affairs at washington [*sic*] for information & action.-

P.M. Butler
[*his signature*]
Ch: Agt.

Fort Gibson
Ch: Nation
6th Feb. 1845

No. 46

[*in faint handwriting below*]

39. No. 8 A1909
Wm Dameron
emigrated in 1838
name not found on Roll of those who were permitted to remove themselves
B2510[*?*]"
[*end of page*]
[*end of document*]

Robert B. Daniel Claim, Cherokee Claims for Commutation of Transportation and Subsistence, Treaty of 1835-36. 1845-55. Special File 154, frames 53-55, Special Files of the Office of Indian Affairs; National Archives micropublication M574, roll 32.

[*first page*]

"Office Indn Affairs
Aug. 19, 1845
56: A1909

T. Hartley Crawford
Commr Indn Aff[*air*]s
Received
22d Augt 1845

Ansd

Rob[t] B. Daniels Claim

M[r] Brown"
[*end of page*]

[*second page*]

"War Department
Office Indian Affairs
August 19. 1845

Sir, I have the honor to enclose a claim of Robert B. Daniel, a Cherokee emigrant, for commutation allowance for two persons. under the treaty of 1835. This claim, with others of a Similar class, was forwarded to this office by the Cherokee Agent on 30. June last.

The facts upon which the claim is founded are Set forth, as you will perceive, in the affidavits of Said Daniel and Susanna Taylor. They are in part, Sustained by the rolls in the office. The name of Robert B. Daniel as the head of a family of four persons, is found on the roll of persons who, having commuted their transportation, were permitted to remove themselves to the Cherokee country west.

I confess I Should be better Satisfied if the facts were all Sustained by Something official, and it had not been without Some little hesitating that I have determined to refer the claim to the Auditor for Settlement, being hardly Satisfied with the Source of the affidavits viz, the claimant himself and his mother in-law, and I do not wish what had been done to be regarded as a"
[*end of page*]

[*third page*]
"precedent for other cases that may be Some what Similar- If, however, the Auditor Shall deem the claim to be duly Supported, and it has not heretofore been paid, I will interpose no objection to its payment, after the requisite examination in his office to ascertain if the claim has not heretofore been paid.

Be pleased to inform me of your decision in the case, that I may make the necessary communication to the proper Agent West.

Very Respectfully
Yr. Ob[t]. Ser[t].
Hartly Crawford.

Gen[l]. Jno. M. M[c]Calla
Second Auditor &c"
[*end of page*]
[*end of document*]

Rance Bird Harris Claim, Cherokee Claims for Commutation of Transportation and Subsistence, Treaty of 1835-36. 1845-55. Special File 154, frames 56-58, Special Files of the Office of Indian Affairs; National Archives micropublication M574, roll 32.

[*first page*]

"B2543
Rance Bird Harris
<u>74:</u>   A1909
claim For Subsistence
Treaty 1835

<u>N°. 23</u>

[*in faint handwriting underneath*]
Disall[d]
[*end of page*]

[*second page*]

"United States To Rance Bird Harris

To transportation for five Slaves $20   100.00
" Subsistence for the Same $33.33 1/3 166. 2/3

We do hereby certify that R. Bird Harris emigrated to this country in the year 1843 and brought with him the above number Slaves.

March 29th 1845.

J.B. Collins [*his signature*]
Joseph Rogers [*his signature*]

Personally appeared before me, R.B. Harris, and makes oath in due form of law that the above account- is just and true, and that he never received any part thereof.

R.B. Harris [*his signature*]

P.M. Butler
Cherokee Agent,

Also the name of J.B. Collins and Jos Rogers was identified before me.

P.M.B.
Ch. Agt."
[*end of page*]

[*third page*]

"Commissioners Office
March 29th 1845,

J.B. Collins and R B Harris appeared before me and were fully identified by Satisfactory evidence to be the proper persons named in the foregoing instrument.

J.T. Mason
[*his signature*]

A true copy from the original now before me
Agency 11 July 1845

P.M. Butler [*his signature*]
Ch. Agt."

[*end of page*]
[*end of document*]

Abstract of Payments Made Under Treaty of 1835, Cherokee Claims for Commutation of Transportation and Subsistence, Treaty of 1835-36. 1845-55. Special File 154, frame 59, Special Files of the Office of Indian Affairs; National Archives micropublication M574, roll 32.

[*Note: this frame only lists the words 'Chiefs', 'Headmen', and 'Warriors'. These words are written several times on this paper.*]

Abstract of Payments Made Under Treaty of 1835, Cherokee Claims for Commutation of Transportation and Subsistence, Treaty of 1835-36. 1845-55. Special File 154, frame 60, Special Files of the Office of Indian Affairs; National Archives micropublication M574, roll 32.

[*Note: This frame is an exact reproduction of frame 62, except that is was microfilmed vertically*]

Abstract of Payments Made Under Treaty of 1835, Cherokee Claims for Commutation of Transportation and Subsistence, Treaty of 1835-36. 1845-55. Special File 154, frame 61, Special Files of the Office of Indian Affairs; National Archives micropublication M574, roll 32.

[page begins]

"A1909 A 1909-45
S.F. 154

A general abstract of payments for commuted transportation and subsistence, under cherokee treaty of 1835-6.

Jn° M McCalla
[*his signature*]
[*illegible*]

Nov [*rip in paper*] [*1*]845

[*in different handwriting on the side near top of paper*]
Chiefs & Headmen Warriors
Head men
Chiefs
Warriors"

[*end of page*]
[*end of document*]

Abstract of Payments Made Under Treaty of 1835, Cherokee Claims for Commutation of Transportation and Subsistence, Treaty of 1835-36. 1845-55. Special File 154, frame 62, Special Files of the Office of Indian Affairs; National Archives micropublication M574, roll 32.

[*Note: frame 62 is a duplicate of frame 63 with the exception that 'Cherokee Payments' is not listed.*]

Abstract of Payments Made Under Treaty of 1835, Cherokee Claims for Commutation of Transportation and Subsistence, Treaty of 1835-36. 1845-55. Special File 154, frame 63, Special Files of the Office of Indian Affairs; National Archives micropublication M574, roll 32.

[*page begins*]

"Cherokee Payments

[*in handwriting on the side*]

(A1909- 45- SP File 154]
Cher"
[*end of page*]
[*end of document*]

James Langley Claim, Cherokee Claims for Commutation of Transportation and Subsistence, Treaty of 1835-36. 1845-55. Special File 154, frames 129-130, Special Files of the Office of Indian Affairs; National Archives micropublication M574, roll 32.

[*first page*]

"B2355
Emigration Cherokee
P.M Butler, ch. agt.
Cherokee agency, 1. Jany 45

Enloses cerrtificate of James W. Deadrick that he did not pay James Langley (lately emigrated) transportaton money- Also power of Atty from Langley to A.D. Wilson to receive & receipt for transportation & subsistence money for him (2)[*?*] and family
Asks for information on the subject.

Rec[d] 6. March 45"
[*end of page*]

[*second page*]

"Cherokee Agency
1st February 1845

Sir,

Enclosed I have the honor to forward you a certificate of James W. Deadrick, Enroling [*sic*] Agent, that he had not paid any thing to- James Langley a cherokee who has lately emigrated to the Cherokee Country west, together with a power of attorney from Langley to A.D. Wilson another Cherokee, authorizing him to receive and receipt for any moneys due him for commutation of-Subsistence.

I have the honor to ask of the Department information upon the Subject of the papers enclosed.

I am Sir Very respectfully Your Ob[t]
Servant

P. M. Butler

[his signature]
Ch. Agt.

Honb[l] T. Hartley Crawford
Com of Ind. Affairs, Washington City."
[end of page]
[end of document]

James Langley Claim, Cherokee Claims for Commutation of Transportation and Subsistence, Treaty of 1835-36. 1845-55. Special File 154, frame 131-134, Special Files of the Office of Indian Affairs; National Archives micropublication M574, roll 32.

[first page]

"Ja[s] Langley
Transportation & Subsistance *[sic]*
A transfer to A.D. Wilson

$213-

[below in upside down handwriting]
B2335"
[end of page]

[second page]

"Know all men by these presents that I do autherise *[sic]* & appoint A D Wilson of the Cherokee Nation to receive & to receipt to the disburseing *[sic]* Agent for my transportation & Subsistence for emigrating four persons in my family to Cherokee Nation West of Arkansas

James Langley
[his signature]

Fort Gibson
Oct. 3rd 1844

Witness

J T Craig
[his signature]"
[end of page]

[third page]

"B2355 James Langley"
[end of page]

[fourth page]

"At the request of James Langley I state that I have not paid any thing toward his transportation to the Cherokee Nation West.

Ja^{s}. W. Deaderick
[his signature]
Enrolling Agent &c

Murphy N. Carolina
Dec. 11th 1843."
[end of page]
[end of document]

Andrew J. Raper Claim, Cherokee Claims for Commutation of Transportation and Subsistence, Treaty of 1835-36. 1845-55. Special File 154, frame 135-136, Special Files of the Office of Indian Affairs; National Archives micropublication M574, roll 32.

[first page]
[Note: there appears to be some writing on this document that is very faint and hard to read. That writing has not been included in this transcription. Please reference original document.]

"B2428.
Emig^{n} Cherokee
P.M. Butler,
ch.agt.

Submists claim of Andrew J. Raper, cherokee emigrant,- for transportation & subsistence money under Cherokee treaty 1835.

Rec^{d} 26. April '45

[*in faint ink below*]
Mr [*could be Wm*] Krebs[?]"
[*end of page*]

[*second page*]

"Personally appeared before me A.J. Raper- a half breed Cherokee & makes oath, that he is the identicel [*sic*] person named in the certificate a [*illegible*] bearing date 18 Jan. 1844 Signed J.W. Deaderick" Enrolling Agt.- & now prays that his Transportation & Subsistence money may be remitted to the U.S. Agent for the Cherokees to be paid him agreeable[?] to the Treaty stipulations- of 1835 & 6-

A J Raper
[*his signature*]

Commissioner's office
March 21. 1845

The above named A.J. Raper appeared before me, signed the above declaration and was identified by Joseph M. Lynch (well known to me) to be the person represented as before declared

John T. Mason
[*his signature*]"

[*end of page*]
[*end of document*]

Andrew J. Raper Claim, Cherokee Claims for Commutation of Transportation and Subsistence, Treaty of 1835-36. 1845-55. Special File 154, frame 137-138, Special Files of the Office of Indian Affairs; National Archives micropublication M574, roll 32.

[*first page*]

"An^{d} J. Raper Certificate"
[*end of page*]

[*second page*
]
"This is to certify that Andrew J. Raper a Cherokee removed from N. Carolina to the Cherokee Nation has received from me no transportation money.

Ja[s]. W. Deaderick
[*his signature*]
Enrolling Agent

Murphey N°. Ca
Jany 18, 1844"
[*end of page*]
[*end of document*]

Ah mah soo yee's Claim, Cherokee Claims for Commutation of Transportation and Subsistence, Treaty of 1835-36. 1845-55. Special File 154, frame 139, Special Files of the Office of Indian Affairs; National Archives micropublication M574, roll 32.

[*page begins*]
[*Note: there appears to be some writing on this document that is very faint and hard to read. That writing has not been included in this transcription. Please reference original document.*]

"1221[?] C73
Ah mah soo ye's Claim. Sub. 39.-
No. 12.-

33 33/100

Delaware Dis[t]
If on inspecting the books it should appear that this man did not- receive his subsistence I would allow $33 33/100[?] under 8th article

B.H. Brewster [*his signature*]
Edward Harden [*his signature*]

Special File No 151
[*end of page*]

[*end of document*]

John Ratcliff Claim, Cherokee Claims for Commutation of Transportation and Subsistence, Treaty of 1835-36. 1845-55. Special File 154, frames 140-145, Special Files of the Office of Indian Affairs; National Archives micropublication M574, roll 32.

[*first page*]
[*Note: there appears to be some writing on this document that is very faint and hard to read. That writing has not been included in this transcription. Please reference original document.*]

"1g[?]- R349 C73
John Ratcliff's Claim Trans. 37 Sub. 37.
No. 61.-"
[*end of page*]

[*second page*]

"The United States
To John Ratcliff D^r

Emigrated in June 1837- Resident of Delaware Dist-

To 11 persons Transportation 20.$ Ea. $220.-
" 11 persons Subsistence for 1 year 33 1/3 Ea. 366. 63

$586.63

John Ratcliff claimant states as follows:
I emigrated in June 1837 having drawn my own transportation and Cherokee family, which consisted of ten in family- and after my arrival in the country I was also paid my subsistence money at 33 1/3$ per head for my cherokee family for the number above named. I owned and brought to this country Eleven slaves, and for which I

was not paid or drawed the transportation money, nor was their subsistence money allowed money after having come into the country- and by the terms of the treaty the Government of the United States had promised to transport and subsist all the Cherokees removed ~~whatever~~ with their families, and the slaves were in my possession, and being necessarily compelled to remove, I believe I am justly entitled to the transportation and subsistence of my slaves;

his
March 27th 1845 John X Ratcliff
mark

Thomas Carey, testifies to the claim of John Ratcliff as follows:
I emigrated a little before the claimant but in the same year, I know he had and brought to this country ten in family of Cherokees, and Eleven slaves. I saw him soon after he came or just coming into the Cherokee Nation and has"
[*end of page*]
[*third page*]
"ever since lived a near neighbor, having settled in a Mile & a half from my residence, the number given in constituted his family at that time I know nothing of his having drawn transportation or subsistence money either in part or whole, all I can testify is the number of his family and having emigrated in 1837.-

March 27th 1845. Thos Carey

Before
G C Washington comr
[*his signature*]"
[*end of page*]

[*fourth page*]

"Additional
Testimony"
[*end of page*]

[*fifth page*]

"Cherokee Agency}
Cherokee nation }

Be it remembered on this 20th day of August 1848. before me R C S Brown, Cherokee Agent, personally came, Charles Ratcliff, son of John Ratcliff who after coming [illegible]. States that he is a Cherokee, & the son of John Ratcliff the claimant.

affiant states, that, his fathers name was (John Ratcliff) & not (John Ralliff) that his father is now dead, and that Letters of Administration in his Estate have been granted to one Lewis-Helterbrand,- affiant states that the reason why his fathers Slaves were not Enrolled, at the time he & his Cherokee family were Enrolled was that he did not, own the slaves, at the time, but before, he Removed from the Eastern, to the Western Cherokee nation his father became the owner, and- possessor of the Eleven slaves, in his application mentioned, affiant states that his father- John Ratcliff, Removed his said Slaves, from the Eastern to the Western Cherokee nation the same time he [*smeared word*]"
[*end of page*]

[*sixth page*]
"Removed his Cherokee family.- that he cannot, positively, state, from whom his father, Recd pay, for the Cherokee part of his family;- but believes, that, a part of it was paid, in the Eastern, or old Cherokee nation, by some agent there before they left the old nation, and part paid in the western Cherokee nation, by some Agent there, affter [*sic*] the arrival of his father and family, in the Western Cherokee nation,

affiant states that he dose [*sic*] not know of any Cherokee by the name of (John Ratliff)

affiant states this father John Ratcliff was a Cherokee had a Cherokee family, Resided for a number of years, in the Eastern Cherokee nation & Enjoyed all the Rights & priveledges [sic] of the Cherokees. & were Recognized by the Cherokee authorities, & that they Removed & settled in the Cherokee nation West. in 1837 where they all permanantly [*sic*] settled for the purpose of

Remaining & have Remained, Except his father who as above stated is dead.

Sworn to & Subscribed before me this day & date above written
Charles Ratcliff
[*his signature*]

RCS Brown Cherokee Agent
[*his signature*]"
[*end of page*]
[*end of document*]

Mary Gilbreath Claim, Cherokee Claims for Commutation of Transportation and Subsistence, Treaty of 1835-36. 1845-55. Special File 154, frames 146-147, Special Files of the Office of Indian Affairs; National Archives micropublication M574, roll 32.

[*first page*]
[*Note: there appears to be some writing on this document that is very faint and hard to read. That writing has not been included in this transcription. Please reference original document.*]

"1211
Mary Galbreath transportation & subsistence
No. 73   C73

~~Rejected~~
BH Brewster [*his signature*]
Edward Harden [*his signature*]

Special File No 154
[*end of page*]

[*second page*]

"United States, To. Mrs. Mary Gilbreath Do
1838 November,

To transportation and subsisting herself and four others, under the provisions of the treaty of 1835-6. at $53 33 1/3 each---- $266.66 2/3[?]

M^{r}. J. Looney states, that M^{rs}. Gilbreath is his step daughter and emigrated West with his negroes when Boudinot came out in 1836 or 37- She brought out four negroes & he does not think she ever received any allowance for transportation or subsistence-

Before me
GC Washington com^{r}.
[*his signature*]

Feby 7th. 1845.

See books at Washington"
[*end of page*]
[*end of document*]

Ah mah soo yee Claim, Cherokee Claims for Commutation of Transportation and Subsistence, Treaty of 1835-36. 1845-55. Special File 154, frames 148-150, Special Files of the Office of Indian Affairs; National Archives micropublication M574, roll 32.

[*first page*]

"10[?]1- 4th: Commission.
Ah tah ka ha gee, states as follows, I came in the same Detachment witht Ah mah soo yee, to the west that in one or two days after the arrival of the Detachments in to the Cherokee Nation West, the U.S. issuing [*inserted*] Commissaries issued Certificates to draw rations and was I present at the place- and to my certain knowledge Ah mah soo yee, or claimant was not there he had started to see some sick relatives, who were [*inserted*] lying sick on or near the Illinois river, some distance from when we had stopt [*sic*]- and did not return untill sometime after the certificates had been issued- Witness [*word smeared*[2]] States further that the issuing Depot was near where

---

[2] It appears that there are only three letters to this word, 'fur'. The word is smeared and is incomplete.

[*inserted*] the Detachment had stopt, and that he (witness) had frequently drawn his rations, but had never seen the claimant draw any rations, and he believes, that said Claimant had never received nor authorised [*sic*] any person to draw for him- and that his rations or its equivalent is still due said Claimant.

his
Feby 19th 1843. Ah tah ka ha gee X
mark

Before G Washington comr.
[*his signature*]

[*it appears that another paper was also microfilmed along with the previous transcription. The transcribed writing is as follows*]

Deleware Dist CN Acy 1843-"
[*end of page*]

[*second page*]
"~~Saline~~ Delaware Dist
22

United States
To Ah, mah, soo, yee Dr

To Subsistence for the year 1839 $33. 33 1/3

Who States that he emigrated to this country in Woffords Detachment in the year 1838, and that he never Received any Subsistence for the year 39 and which he believes that he is entitled to the Amt of thirty ~~tha~~ three dollars & thirty three cents as that is the amount allowed for one year Subsistence and states further, that soon after his arrival into the Cherokee Nation West, he had gone off from his Detachment to visit some sick persons where he remained several days and after returning to his Detachment, certificates for drawing rations had already ~~received~~ ~~[*illegible*]~~ ~~Certificates~~ been issued by the U.S. Commissaries, and that his wife had also received a Certificate for her own rations, but he had not received his, as the Commissaries had left the place he had no opportunity to ask for or obtain his Certificate- and therefore could draw no rations with it and has never received nor authorised [*sic*] any person to receive his rations- and believes he is justly entitled to the same-

Feby 19th 1845.

his
Ah mah soo X yee
mark

Before
GC Washington com.r "
[*his signature*]

[*third page*]

"10[?]1- 4th: Commission.

Ah tah ka ha gee, States as follows,
I came in the same Detachment with Ah mah soo yee, to the West that in one or two days after the arrival of the Detachments into the Cherokee Nation West, the U.S. issuing Commissaries issued Certificates to draw rations and was present at the place- and to my certain knowledge Ah mah soo yee, or claimant was not there he had started to see some sick relatives, who were [*inserted*] lying sick on or near the Illinois river some distance from where we had stopt [*sic*]- and did not return until sometime after the Certificates had been issued- Witness [*word smeared*[3]] States further that the issuing Depot was near where [*inserted*] the Detachment had stopt [*sic*], and that he (witness) had frequently drawn his rations, but had never seen the Claimant draw any rations, and he believes, that said Claimant had never received nor authorised [*sic*] any person to draw for him- and that his rations or its equivalent is still due said Claimant.

his
Ah tah ka ha gee X
mark

Before G Washington com.r

---

[3] It appears that there are only three letters to this word, 'fur'. The word is smeared and is incomplete.

Deleware Dis[t] CN Acy 1843-
This is to certify that Ah=ma=soo=ee is one of the late emigrants and came in my detachment who says he received no rations of provisions [*inserted*] after our arrival in this country
JD. Wafford as con[d] of a detachment &c &c
[*his signature*]

Before me GC W[*ashingto*]n [*his signature*][4]"
[*end of page*]
[*end of document*]

John Barns Claim, Cherokee Claims for Commutation of Transportation and Subsistence, Treaty of 1835-36. 1845-55. Special File 154, frames 151-158, Special Files of the Office of Indian Affairs; National Archives micropublication M574, roll 32.

[*first page*]

"Emigration Cherokee
M41
Ja[s]. McKisick
Chero. Agent, Jan, 26/47
End[?], claim &c, of John Barns, for commutation of subsisbence for 6 ½ months

Recv[d]. Feb. 19. 1847.

[*in faint handwriting below*]
Civilization

---

[4] It appears that this statement by J.D. Wafford was written on a separate piece of paper and then microfilmed on top of the Ah tah ka ha gee statement. There is additional writing below this certification by J.D. Wafford, but it is missing from this microfilmed frame; it was either cut off, torn off, or was folded when this claim was microfilmed. The original file should be searched to locate this document in order to find additional information.

[*end of page*]

[*second page*]

"Cherokee Agency
26th January 1847

Sir

I have the honor herewith to enclose the claim of John Barnes a cherokee, for commutation of subsistence for Six months and a half, with Seven in family, The proof was taken by Cherokee Judges, and of whom it will be seen, has identified the number in family, designating their six Pages

The case is respectfully submitted

Verry Respectfully Your Obt Servt
Jas M[*c*]Kisick
[*his signature*]
Cherokee Agent

Col William Medill}
Comr Indian Affairs}
Washington City }"
[*end of page*]
[*third page*]

"<u>John Barnes's</u>
Subsistence <u>claim</u>

[*in faint handwriting upside down*]
M41"
[*end of page*]

[*fourth page*]

"United States
To John Barnes a cherokee Dr

To Subsisting himself & family seven in number from the [*illegible*] 1st May 1832 to the middle of Novr at the rates of $33.33 cts per year

John Barnes being sworn states that his residence in the old Cherokee Nation East was on the Hightower river about one mile below Columbus in the limits of the state of Tennessee, And that he Emigrated himself & family from the Said place some time in the spring of 1834 as well as he can recollect- And that he was paid by the Agent for the cherokees East Eighteen Dollars Each for his family as that was the amount allowed to the cherokees at that time who Transported themselves to the Agency west- and that he found his own boat & transported himself & family, and when he left- the cherokee Agency East he was told by the Agent to try and report himself to cherokee agent west by the first of May so as to draw money for Twelve subsistance [*sic*] but in consequence of a great deal of sickness on the river that year he & his family were detained along on the river and at the first of May he landed his boat about Two miles above Little rock, and had to scuffle along the best way he could with his sick family- and it was some time in august before he arrived into the Cherokee Nation with his family at the place where he now lives on salisaw in Flint District and he had to buy corn and meat Until some time in Nov. at which he the said Barnes got able to go & report himself and family to the cherokee agent west he then drawed [*sic*] rations from that time to the"
[*end of page*]

[*fifth page*]

"first of May 1845 and that he has been paid the balance of the Twelve months subsistance [*sic*] which he was Entitled to by Treaty

his
John Barnes X
mark

Sworn to & subscribed before me this 2nd may 1845

Jay Hicks
[*his signature*]
J, D, C

Meredith Roberts being sworn states that he was staying on the place where Mr. Barnes now lives on Salisaw in Flint District when Mr Barnes arrived there some time in august 1834 and knows that

Mr John Barnes had his corn & meat to buy, and did buy it from his neighbors Until some time in Novr at which time Mr Barnes reported himself to the agent and Drawed [*sic*] ~~to~~ rations about four or five months as well as well as he can recollect and further says that he has lived a close Neighbor to Barnes ever since & does not know that Barnes has ever been paid by any of the agents of the govt for subsisting his family the lenght [*sic*] of time he has charged in his acct against the United states

M. Roberts
[*his signature*]

Sworn to & subscribed before me 2nd May 1845

Jay Hicks
[*his signature*]
J.D.C"

[*end of page*]

[*sixth page*]

"Wm Pettit being sworn states that he ~~lived on~~ owned the place where Mr Barnes now lives at the time Barnes arrived in the Nation with his family some time in august 1832 and that the said Barnes bought the place of him and still remains on the same place- and that he let Mr Barnes have provisions alone on his own credit Until some time in october there was arrangements made for him & his family to draw rations.

William Petitt
[*his signature*]

Sworn to & submitted before me 6th May 1845

Jay Hicks
[*his signature*]
J, D, C

~~$15.29~~
~~107.03~~ $125 75[*?*]"
[*end of page*]

[*seventh page*]

"John Barns

[*in faint handwriting upside down*]
M41"
[*end of page*]

[*eighth page*]

"Cherokee Nation}
Flint District }

Personally appeared before me J. George Chambers Judge of the afore said District. John Barns who being duly Sworn in due form of law states that he enrolled and amigrated [*sic*] to this country in 1833 under Hugh Montgomery who was then agent for the Cherokees East, and he the Said agent never give him [*sic*] enrolling Certificates, of which he was entitled too [*sic*].

his
John Barns +
mark

Sworn to & Subscribed before me this 15th January 1847
George Chambers. J., D, Ct
[*his signature*]

John Barns. Family

1. John Barns
2. Tenesse Barns
3. William Barns- - Ages- 24 & 6 mo
4. Susan Barns- " 23- 2- "
5. Margaret Barns- " 18- 10- "
6. Nancy Barns- " 20-- 6- "
7. Thomas Barns- " 16 ----

Two boys }
three girls }

I do hereby certify that John Barns [*inserted*] has the number ~~of~~ five family as written in the above- Given[*?*] from [*illegible*] my hand this 15th Jany

George Chambers J, D, Ct
[*his signature*]
J,D,C"

[*end of page*]
[*end of document*]

Night Killer Claim, Cherokee Claims for Commutation of Transportation and Subsistence, Treaty of 1835-36. 1845-55. Special File 154, frames 159-161, Special Files of the Office of Indian Affairs; National Archives micropublication M574, roll 32.

[*first page*]

"Emigration Cherokee
B.281.
R.C.S. Brown,
July 22, 1848,
In relation to bal. cl^{d} by Night Killer, & Subsistence & transp^{n} &c.

Rec^{d}. 22 Aug. 1848.
Ans$^{d[?]}$ Aug 23/48"
[*end of page*]

[*second page*]

"To Wm Medill Esqr
Commissioner of Indian Affairs
Washington City DC"
[*end of page*]

[*third page*]

"Cherokee Agency
July 22 1848

To W[m] Midell Esq

Sir

I am called upon you by Night Killer a Cherokee requesting of me to write you, on the subject of his Claim for Subsistence, for himself and family, M[r] Night Killer when he imigrated [*sic*] to the Indian Country west procured, a certificate of Enrolment from Gen[l] N Smith, Superintendant [*sic*] of the Cherokees removal [*illegible*], the East, when he arrived in this country, he presented it to Cap[t] Stephenson, the Disbursing agent and derived from Cap[t] Stephenson, and at the same time, and at the request of Cap[t] Stephenson, gave him Gen[l] N Smiths certificate, as the Books are all in the Department, I must respectfully ask [*th*]at they be Examined and the balance If any be found Due to M[r] Night Killer, be forwarded to the proper office to be Paid over.

Respectfully Your ob[t] Sr
R C S Brown
[*his signature*]
Cherokee Agent"

[*end of page*]
[*end of document*]

Claims of Isaac Goddard, John R. Blythe, and Nancy J. Fields, Cherokee Claims for Commutation of Transportation and Subsistence, Treaty of 1835-36. 1845-55. Special File 154, frames 162-164, Special Files of the Office of Indian Affairs; National Archives micropublication M574, roll 32.

[*first page*]

"Emigration Cherokee
B.284
RCS Brown
July 26. 1848.
In relation to Sub. claims of Isaac Goddard, Jno. R. Blythe, & Nancy J. Fields, &c.

Claims allowed- see letter to S.M Rutherford ap[l] 16, 1849

Rec[d] 22 Aug[t] 1848

[*in faint handwriting below*]
Civilization"
[*end of page*]

[*second page*]

"To. W. Medill Esqr
Commissioner of Indian Affairs
Washington City, DC"
[*end of page*]

[*third page*]

"Cherokee Agency
July 26th 1848.

To W Medill Esqr
Commissioner of Indian Affairs
Washington City

Sir

I write you at the request of the Several persons here, to Wit" Isaac Goddard, John R. Blythe, and Nancy J. Fields, Each of whom State that in the Summer of 1845, they gave to Governor Benton their certificates of N. Smith Superintendant [*sic*] of Cherokee Removal, to have their Subsistence money forwarded on.

Since which time they have not heard a word, about it, they are fearful that their claims have not, been presented to the Department, or they would have heard from them, in this, This Letter is [*illegible*] to make the inquiry & Elicit an answer.

Verry [*sic*] Respectfully
Your Ob[t] Sv[t]
R C S. Brown
[*his signature*]
Cherokee Agent"

[*end of page*]
[*end of document*]

Charles Vickery Claim, Cherokee Claims for Commutation of Transportation and Subsistence, Treaty of 1835-36. 1845-55. Special File 154, frames 165-167, Special Files of the Office of Indian Affairs; National Archives micropublication M574, roll 32.

[*first page*]
[*Note: there appears to be some writing on this document that is very faint and hard to read. That writing has not been included in this transcription. Please reference original document.*]

Emigration Cherokee
B.311.
RCS Brown
Cher Ag^{t}. Sept 28, '48
In relation to claim of Charles Vickery for tran$^{sp.}$ & subsistence &c

[*in faint writing below*]
No such claim has been rec^{d} in this office- an individual of this name was Paid in 2 qr 1838- a commutation of Trans & sub for 2.

Rec^{d}. 23 Oct. 1848
Ans^{d} O[*c*]t 26/48"
[*end of page*]

[*second page*]

To). W. Medill Esq$^{r.}$
Commissioner of Indian affairs.
Washington City D.C."
[*end of page*]

[*third page*]

"Cherokee Agency
Sept. 28th 1848

To) W. Medill Esqr.
Commissioner of Indian Affairs
Washington City D.C.

Sir

I am called on by Charles Vickery, a Cherokee, to Enquire [*sic*] relative to his claim, for Transportation & subsistance [*sic*], his claim he states was proven up, some years since before Genl Mason, when in this country as Indian commissioner, & was placed in the hands of Col Sta[*????*]an for collection, since which time, it has not been heard from.

Will you be pleased to Give such information as in your power & oblige &c

Verry Respectfully
Your Obt Servt
R C S Brown
[*his signature*]
Cherokee Agent."

[*end of page*]
[*end of document*]

Letter from Samuel M. Rutherford to William Medill regarding Cherokee Claims, Cherokee Claims for Commutation of Transportation and Subsistence, Treaty of 1835-36. 1845-55. Special File 154, frames 168-169, Special Files of the Office of Indian Affairs; National Archives micropublication M574, roll 32.

[*first page*]

"~~S??pd~~ Emig[*r*]ation Cherokee
R264
S.M. Rutherford
May 31, 1848
Ackg. letter of 26 Apl. accompg. Commutation claims &c. &c

Recd. 3d[*?*] June 1848
[*in fant ink below with a checkmark*]

File"
[*end of page*]

[*second page*]

"Choctaw Agency
Aug 31st 1848

Sir

I have the honor to acknowledge the receipt of yours of the 26th Ult. Accompanied by certain claims for commutation of removal, and Subsistence, under Cherokee treaty of 1835-36;

The above claims[*?*] with the funds when accrued, will be turned over to Judge Brown Agent for the Cherokees, with particular instructions in regards to the vouchers which will be required for the disbursement thus made.

Very respectfully
Your Obt. Servt.
S.M. Rutherford
[*his signature*]
Actg Supt. W. Ty.

Hon^l W. Medill
Comm^r Omd Affr^s
Washington City D.C."
[*end of page*]
[*end of document*]

Letter from Samuel M. Rutherford to William Medill regarding Cherokee Claims, Cherokee Claims for Commutation of Transportation and Subsistence, Treaty of 1835-36. 1845-55. Special File 154, frames 170-171, Special Files of the Office of Indian Affairs; National Archives micropublication M574, roll 32.

[*first page*]

"Emgⁿ Settler Cherokee
R.304
Saml M. Rutherford

Aug. 4. 1848
Transmits 19. claims for commutation &c. of Cherokee Indians-
Also letter from Hon. R.C.S. Brown ag[t]. relating to them.

Rec[d] Sep[t]. 1. 1848
See letter to Rutherford 10 April 1849.

[*writing below in faded ink*]
civilization
1-"
[*end of page*]

[*second page*]

Choctaw Agency
August 4th 1848

Sir

Herewith enclosed you will find 19 claims for commutation of Transportation and Subsistence in favor of certain Cherokee Indians, also a letter from the Hon[l] RCS Brown their Agent in which particular reference is made to each of Said claimants

Very respectfully
Your Obt. Servt.
S.M. Rutherford
[*his signature*]
Actg Supt. W. Ty

Hon[l] W[m] Medill
Comm[s] Ind Affr[s]
Washington City DC"
[*end of page*]
[*end of document*]

Hiram Moody Claim, Cherokee Claims for Commutation of Transportation and Subsistence, Treaty of 1835-36. 1845-55. Special File 154, frames 172-174, Special Files of the Office of Indian Affairs; National Archives micropublication M574, roll 32.

[*first page*]

"R304
Hiram Moodys Claim against the United States
Suspended.
X
new Claim"
[*end of page*]

[*second page*]

"Cherokee Agency West

Be it known that on this 12th day of July 1848, before RCS Brown, Cherokee Agent, personally came Hiram Moodey, a white- with a Cherokee wife- who being duly sworn states, that he was married to his wife in the Eastern Cherokee nation & Remained there for some months with his wife, that they were Recognized by the Cherokee Authorities, as Cherokees, and Entitled to the usual priviled[g]es of other Cherokees, affiant states that his wife left the Eastern Cherokee nation, with what was called the Ross Removels [*sic*] & was attached to Judge James Browns detachment, & has ever since the arrival of said detachment been in the Weste[*rn*] Cherokee nation & have permnatly [*sic*] settled there, with the intentio[*n*] of Remaining,

affiant states that in some short time after he and his wife arrived here they drew rations, consisting of Beef & corn to a small amount, together [*with*] some salt but has never drew any Rations since, nor has he, nor his wife, ever, Rec^{d} any Commutation for subsistence from the united states, the Cherokee people or other authority, whatever save the small amount of Beef & corn, & salt, above mentioned. affiant states that he ~~believed~~ is informed that"
[*end of page*]

[*third page*]

"Books, of the Commissary, who Issued at the time have all been filed in some one of the offices, of the wa[*r*] department, where they can only be Examined by the proper officers there & preys [*sic*] that such Examination be made as will, Enable the applicant to Receive the small amount due himself & wife- as a Balance, of their years Subsistance,

his
Hiram X Moody
mark

sworn to & subscribed before me}
this day and date above written }

RCS Brown
[*his signature*]
Cherokee Agent"
[*end of page*]
[*end of document*]

J.B. Collins/Rance B. Harris Claim Cover Sheet, Cherokee Claims for Commutation of Transportation and Subsistence, Treaty of 1835-36. 1845-55. Special File 154, frame 175, Special Files of the Office of Indian Affairs; National Archives micropublication M574, roll 32.

[*page begins*]
"R304
J.B. Collins claim for Subsistence and Transportation to be forwarded to the Department, July 1848.

[*underneath in different ink*]
Claim of Rance Bird Harris-

X
Ready to Enclose to commissioner of Indian affairs
New Claim"
[*end of page*]
[*end of document*]

List of Claims Sent to Commissioners of Indian Affairs, Cherokee Claims for Commutation of Transportation and Subsistence, Treaty of 1835-36. 1845-55. Special File 154, frames 176-182, Special Files of the Office of Indian Affairs; National Archives micropublication M574, roll 32.

[*first page*]

"R304
List of Claims Sent to Commissioners of Indian Affairs ~~[*illegible*] a office~~ for allowance .
[*end of page*]

[*second page*]
"The following are a list of Claims for Transportation and Subsistence, Some of which are of this Sixteen Claims forwarded to this Agency for further proof, on the 18th of March 1848, and Some of which were returned to this office, 25th June 1846, and also Some few entirely new, namely

1st Mrs Margarett Morgan,

In this case I have retakin [*sic*] the Evidence of Mrs Morgan, Coln George Lowrey Second Chief in the Nation, and a gentleman of high and unimpeachible[*?*] character, and also the Evidence of John Benge, another Gentleman of high respectability, they have each, Somewhat enlarged on their former Testimony, and hope they have so well sustained the Testimony of Mrs Morgan, together with her good character for truth and veracity, that her claim will no longer be with held from her, I have also taken the Evidence of Susan Fallen, of this Lady I cannot Speak for, know nothing of her. Yet she is one of the Individuals that Mrs Morgan removed to this country with her, and realy [*sic*] shewed [*sic*] a disposition not to Testify in the case, It is believed that she could have identified every Indian included in Mrs Morgans application, had it not been for feelings of prejudice, which she evidently showed at the time, her evidence was takin [*sic*] down, her Testimony however I conceive goes a great way towards proving the whole of Mrs Morgans Claim, Several of the Persons Enumerated in Mrs Morgans Claim, they are Scattered, about over the various parts of the Nation, and would

cause a Travel of from 150 to 300 Miles, to collect them all at the Agency, so as to procure proper release from them as to the Transportation and Subsistence, and the applicant would prefer looseing [sic] the amount of the Claim, rather than be put to further Trouble and vexation about them, and on this state of [*illegible*] can, Submits the matter for your cocnsideration, She is satisfied with the allowances made to Nelly and Susan, Fallen, as they have each acknowledged that she Mrs Morgan,"
[*end of page*]

[*third page*]
"Removed them from the Old Nation, to this Nation and that they could not have got here, had it not been for her Kindness, and each of them, have paid her $20.00 for removing them, Mrs Morgan Still contends however that she should be Entitled to Transportation for her Son, G.W. Morgan, that She removed him to this country, and that he promised to remain with her, but so it was, he returned to the old Nation in Some Short time then after, to have the balance of the family ready to remove to the West, but in some short time thereafter he was in Washington City, and various other places in the East, and finally was appointed in the United States Army, and went to Mexico, all of which Mrs Morgan, had no control over, her Son however, (GW Morgan) writes her from Mexico, that on his return, he is coming to reside with her, a Larger portion of the above, I am a ware is not strictly Evidence, but is rather a history of the case, that may give it such insights[*?*] as it may be entitled to,

From my own knowledge of Mrs Morgan, I am perfectly satisfied that she is entitled to all she has claimed for except the Mrs Fallens, to whom allowances have already been made, I have known her ever since in the country and I have at no time heard her veracity doubted. I have known Col^n^ George Lowrey the 2nd Chiefs in the Nation for 30 Years and unhesitatingly say I would believe every word, that he would Testify to, I have also been acquainted with John Benge. Since in ths country, Say 8 or 10 Years and from my knowledge of him together with his character I would be bound to believe any Statement he would make and although Mrs Morgans [*illegible*] claim is not Litterally [*sic*] proven up, I am of opinion that she has shown so much Equity[?] in it, that it will without hesitation be paid

2nd Mrs Minerva Lea,

In this case, the Testimony is as you required in the Instructions, and should doubtless be allowed"
[*end of page*]

[*fourth page*]
"3rd Brice Hilter Brand,

In this case, I am of opinion, that the Evidence is so Specifically taken down, that it will not admit of a Doubt, and he should be paid for Subsistence.

4th Wm J McCoy.

The additonal Testimony in this case It seems to me will entitle the Applicant to an allowance, with the applicant and witness I am not acquainted.

5th Henry Morton

There are three additional depositions Taken in this case, and it Seems to me to be proven, (Parties all Strangers)

6th Livingston Garratt.

The additonal Testimony of three witnesses To wit. James A Thompson, a white man, well known to me to be a man of high Respectable Standing,- Joseph M. Lynch, a Cherokee of Respectable Standing and John Williams, a whiteman, with an Indian family, who of respectability, the evidence of these witnesses will entitle the applicant to his Transportation and Subsistence.

7th Ellis Fallen.

Has filed additional Testimony, which will Entitle him to Transportation and Subsistence of the witnesses herein, I know nothing.

8th Timothy M Walker

In this case the additional Testimony is from a Respectable Source, his claim will Doubtless be allowed.

over."

[*end of page*]

[*fifth page*]
"9th Adam Bible

Mr Bible has filed some additional Testimony of himself and Mr Martin, neither of which do I know, or have heard any thing of their character.

10th Lydia Harnage

This is one of the claims, sent back, 25th June 1846 for her additional Testimony. If Books of Agent Vanhorn shows a balance in her favour, she will be entitled to it.

11th Nancy Levit

This is one of the claims Sent back 25th June 1846, sends her additonal Testimony, and shews [sic] herself to be Entitled to Transportation & Subsistence for one year $53. 33 1/3/100-

12th Nancy Daniel & others

The Deposition of Thomas Daniel together with N. Smiths accompanying Statement will entitle the applicants to their pay, If all should stand fair upon the Books at the Department.

13th Betsy Covel & Eliza Wolf,

Have sent additional Testimony which I Submit without remark, further than the persons whom Testified, are verry Respectable, but the circumstances under which they came I am not prepared to say a word about.

14th Heirs of Nancy Harlin

This is a new claim, and seems to be well proven up by Mrs Elizabeth Medley, who is represented as being highly respectable, and Entitled credit on oath also the affadavit [*sic*] of Stand Watie, a highly respectable & Talented Cherokee,"
[*end of page*]

[*sixth page*]

"15th Mrs Elizabeth Browns Claim

This is the first claim that I have had any thing to do with, and took the Evidence of E. Brown, Jas Brown Sr and James Brown Jr. with out having Examined the Laws or instructions , I have since met with Robertson Brown, son of Elizabeth, and taken his Testimony, all which is herewith submitted, (I was personally present at the residence of Mrs Elizabeth Brown and saw all of the persons in her Afft. Ennumerated [*sic*], have no hesitation in recommending that her claim for Transportation , & Subsistence, should be paid, If I had the instructions pryor [*sic*] to takeing [*sic*] the afft. Of E. Brown, I should have taken in addition the Testimony of (Rachel McIntosh) who is named in Mrs Browns afft, as she was sitting by and assenting to her name being placed in Mrs Browns application, and it being a distance of 55 Miles form the Agency to Mrs Browns, I have determined to risk the claim as it now stands, and will remark here that James Brown Sr and James Brown Jr. are both Gentlemen of good Standing in community and entitled to much credit, Mrs E Brown and her son, Robertson altho [*sic*] Partially ~~and~~? Strangers [*illegible*] I [*illegible*] they are regarded as highly respectable, Industrious and honest, and would respectfully recommend that her claim be allowed.

16th Hemden[?] Moody

This is a new claim and will depend on the Books in your office whether he has received in money or Rations his Twelve months Subsistence, I would remark however that Mr Moody is a verry [*sic*] respectable man.

17th Adah Adair

This is a new claim, made out by Coln Wattie Adair, an Indian Countryman and seems"

[*end of page*]

[*seventh page*]

"to be well done, the witnesses are known to me as verry [*sic*] Respectable men, and the claim should be allowed.

18th J.B. Collins

This claim was handed me a few days since It seems to have approved of by, J.T. Mason, as you see from the Endorsement on the Back of the claim, I send this paper not knowing what to do with it.

19 Luther Crutchfield
Has Sustained his claim with evidence which is Represented as coming form a Respectable Source, and I suppose it Should be allowed him.

RCS Brown
[*his signature*]
Cherokee Agent"

[*end of page*]
[*end of document*]

Adah Adair Claim, Cherokee Claims for Commutation of Transportation and Subsistence, Treaty of 1835-36. 1845-55. Special File 154, frames 183-191, Special Files of the Office of Indian Affairs; National Archives micropublication M574, roll 32.

[*first page*]

"R304
D268
Adah Adair
To} Claim against the United Stats for Transportation & subsistance [*sic*] for Eleven persons
Suspended.
Additional Testimony
X
Complete
new Claim."
[*end of page*]

[*second page*]

"Cherokee nation west}
Cherokee Agency }

Be it known that I R.CS Brown United states, Agent to the Cherokee Tribe of Indians, west do hereby Certify that Dell Foreman whose name is signed to the Four several foregoing affidavits of 1st Adah Adai[*r*] 2ndly J. Lafayette Adair. 3rdly Andrew Adair and Fourthly Jesse Mayfield; as Chief Justice of the Supreme Court, of the Cheroke[*e*] nation, is now, and was at the time of the signing the Same, Chief Justice of the Supreme Court of the Said Cherokee nation as aforesaid and that full faith, and Credit, it is due to all of his official acts, and that his signature to Each of the foregoing [*illegible*], affidavits is genuine

In testimoney [*sic*] I RCS Brown Cherokee Agent as

aforsaid [*sic*] have hereunto set my hand, and signed my name officially this 8th day of July AD 1848

R.C.S. Brown
[*his signature*]
Cherokee Agent"

[end of page]

[*third page*]

The United States
To J. Lafayette Adair D.-
For transportation of Eleven in family from the Eastern to the western Nation of Cherokee Indians in the month of November & December 1847 at twenty dollars a head $220.00
For Subsistence for Eleven persons one year from the 14th December 1847 at thirty three dollars ~~per head~~ and thirty three cents per head 366.63

$586.63

[*end of page*]

[*fourth page*]

"Cherokee Nation

Be it known that on the Eighteenth day of June Eighteen hundred and forty eight (1848) Came before me D.M. Foreman Chief Justice of the Supreme Court of the Nation aforesaid, Adah Adair Widow of Samuel Adair dec[d] Who was a Cherokee of the half blood- makes oath in due form, Saith, that her late husband before his death Appointed J Lafayette Adair as head of the family and he has So been considered by the family ever Since, and we allow him to have the entire control and management of all domestic concerns So fare [*sic*] as a male is entitled to governe-. That our family consists of Eleven, myself, three Cherokee children, the children of Samuel Adair dec[d] one male and three females, Seven negro Slaves two males and five females, that we never have Received : Compensation for transportation or Subsistance [*sic*] or either, nor was She or any part of the family at the expense of the Goverment [*sic*] Subsisted in kind or otherwise- that we came West"

[*end of page*]

[*fifth page*]

"with the expectation of remaining citizens of the Cherokee Nation west- and that they never were before removed at the expense of the United States or the Cherokee people, or by any other who was paid therefor.

Sworn to and Subscribed before me, the date above written.

her
Adah + Adair
mark

D.M. Foreman
[*his signature*]
C.J.S.Ct."
[*end of page*]

[*sixth page*]

"...Cherokee Nation

Be it known that on the seventeenth day of June Eighteen hundred & forty eight (1848) Came before me D.M. Foreman Chief Justice of Supreme Court of the nation of aforesaid J L. Adair- a quarter blood Cherokee- makes oath in due form and Saith that he Emigrated from the Eastern Nation to the Western Na. in the year (1847) Eighteen hundred & forty seven Starting from the East 3rd November, that he arrived in the West the 14th December, that he Emigrated himself at this own expense, that it was his intention to have enrolled and emigrated at the expense of the Goverment [*sic*] but was unable to do So their being no enrolling Agent at the time in the Eastern Nation- that his Father was a Cherokee of the half blood by the name of Samuel Adair and his mother a white woman- that they never Removed west before, that they never Received Compensation for transportation or Subsistance [*sic*] or either- nor was his or any part of the family at the expense of the Goverment [*sic*] Subsisted in kind or otherwise- that our family consists of a mother & three Cherokee"
[*end of page*]

[*seventh page*]

"Children one male and three females Seven (7) negroe [*sic*] Slaves two males and five females, that we emigrated with the intention and expectation of locating perminently [*sic*] in the Nation West- and that they never were before Removed at the expense of the United States or the Cherokee people or by any other who was paid therefor.

Sworn to and subscribed before me the date above written.

J Lafayette Adair
[*his signature*]

D.M. Foreman
[*his signature*]
C.J.S.Ct."
[*end of page*]

[*eigth page*]

"...Cherokee Nation.

Be it known, that on the 11th day of June, Eighteen hundred & forty eight (1848) Came before me D.M. Foreman Chief Justice of the Supreme Court aforesaid Andrew Adair- Who States on Oath that he is acquainted with J Lafayette Adair his mother and two Sisters, that his mother is a white woman, the widow of Samuel Adair dec[d] Who was a Cherokee of the half blood that J Lafayette Adair and his two sisters are Cherokees of the quarter blood- that they have seven negroes and they arrived in the Western Nation of Cherokees, about the (14th) fourteenth of December last- and he believes it is their intention of remaining Citizens of the Cherokee Nation West- And that they have never before Removed at the expence [*sic*] of the United States or the Cherokee people, or any other who was paid therefor.

Sworn to and Subscribed before me the date above written.

Andrew Adair
[*his signature*]

DM Foreman
[*his signature*]
C.J.S.Ct."
[*end of page*]

[*ninth begins*]

"Cherokee Nation.

Be it known that on the seventeenth day of June Eighteen hundred and forty eight (1848) Came before me D.M. Foreman Chief Justice of the Supreme Court of Nation aforesaid Jesse Mayfield, makes Oath in due form, Saith, that he was in the Eastern Nation in the fall of Eighteen & forty seven (1847) and that he left for the Western Nation on, or about the third of November and that J Lafayette Adair with the family Started about the same time: that J Lafayette Adair family consists of the Mother and three Cherokee Children- one male, and three females, Seven Negroes, two males and five females- that we got in Company a short time after we Set out from the eastern Nation, and traveled in Company together until we arrived in the Western Nation- which was about the fourteenth (14th) of December 1847-

Sworn to, and Subscribed before me, the date above written.

DM Foreman
[*his signature*]
CJ.S.Ct."
[*end of page*]
[*end of document*]

Jesse Mayfield
[*his signature*]

Letter from Samuel H. Rutherford regarding Cherokeec claims, Cherokee Claims for Commutation of Transportation and Subsistence, Treaty of 1835-36. 1845-55. Special File 154, frames 192-193, Special Files of the Office of Indian Affairs; National Archives micropublication M574, roll 32.

[*page begins*]

"Emg[n] Cherokee
<u>Letter</u>
R. 305
Sam[l] M. Rutherford
Aug. 9. 1848.
Inclg 5 claims for commuta[n] of transp[n] & subsistence of Cherokees with descriptive list by Agent Brown.
Rec[d] Sep[t] 1. 1848
See letter to Sup[t] Rutherford 16 April '49
Civilization [*in faint ink*]"
[*end of page*]

[*page begins*]

"Choctaw Agency
Augt. 9th 1848

Sir

Enclosed you will receive 5 Claims of certain Cherokee Indians for commutation of Subsistence and Transportation also descriptive list in which they are particularly refered [*sic*] to by Agent Brown.

Respectfully Your Ob[t] Servt.
S.M. Ru[*t*]herford
[*his signature*]
Actg Supt. W. Ty.

Hon[l] W[m] Medill
Comm[s] Ind Affr[s]
Washingtn city."
[*end of page*]
[*end of document*]

Sally Bark's Claim, Cherokee Claims for Commutation of Transportation and Subsistence, Treaty of 1835-36. 1845-55. Special File 154, frames 194-196, Special Files of the Office of Indian Affairs; National Archives micropublication M574, roll 32.

[first page]

"R305
Sally Barks Claim.
X"
[*end of page*]

[*second page*]
"Cherokee Agency west

Be it remembered that on this 1st day of August 1848 before me R.C.S. Brown Cherokee Agent personally came Sally Bark, a Cherokee Woman who being duly sworn states that she is a Cherokee, that she was raised in & Resided in the Easter[*n*] Cherokee nation, until in the year 1838 or thereabouts, that her family were all Recognized as Cherokee by the authorities, & were Entitled to such priveledgs [*sic*] as other Cherokees, that in the year of 1838 affiant states that she together with her family & various others were enrolled as a family, & affiant was at the head of the family, her recollection is that there were about Thirty (30) in number,- (only Eighteen, however, Emigrated to the Cherokee nation west with said affiant) & for these Eighteen, peron [*sic*] affiant states, that the proper agent in the East paid her their Transportation money be fore [*sic*] they left the old nation, affiant states the [*sic*] she & her family of Eighteen are well in the Cherokee nation west in year of 1839 & in some short time there-after, Reported herself & family to the proper agent then at Fort Gibson, she believes to Copl Stephenson, who was at the time the proper office to report to, & that he- Copl Stephenson, or the agent whoever he was paid her one hundred dollars in part pay for the Subsistance [*sic*] of her self & family & Required of affiant Leave with hi[*m*] her[*?*] Certificate of Removal From Gen[l] N. Smith" [*page ends*]

[*third page*]

"and to call Every three months, & Receive the Balance of her Subsistance [*sic*] money- affiant States that at the End of three months, She called again, on the Agent, Gov[r] Stokes who in formed [*sic*] her, that he was ordered, not [*to*] pay out anymore money to the Indians, owing [*to*] some difficulties that had taken place among the Indians, (affiant states this was shortly after the killing of the Ridges & Boudinot,) affiant states that she has not at any time called on any agent to have the matter [*illegible*]

affiant states that her own immediate family, after she arrived & settled here consisted only of (nine persons) (9) that she & ~~they~~ her family have Remained here ever since, & are perminantly [*sic*]- settled, and are Recongnized [*illegible*] as Cherokees, & Entitled to the same privileges of other Cherokees,- affiant states that, she only claims subsistance [*sic*] for her immediate family of nine, after deducting the one hundred dollars off which was paid as above stated, & that the amt. found due may be forwarded to the proper officer in the west with orders to have it immediately paid over to her.

Affiant most positively states she never has Rec[d]. from the united states, the Cherokee people, or from any other authority, whatever, any Commutation for Subsistance [*sic*] Either in money or in kind Except the $100.00- here in mentioned.

Sworn to & Subscribed before me
this date above
RCS Brown
[*his signature*]
Cherokee Agent"
[*end of page*]
[*end of document*]

her
Sally X Bark
mark

Richard Foreman Claim, Cherokee Claims for Commutation of Transportation and Subsistence, Treaty of 1835-36. 1845-55. Special File 154, frames 197-201, Special Files of the Office of Indian Affairs; National Archives micropublication M574, roll 32.

[first page]

"R305
Rich[d] Formans apt}D.224
United States
S.F 154
X"
[*end of page*]

[*second page*]

"Cherokee Agency West
Cherokee Nation

Be it Remembered that on this 12th day of July 1848 personally before me Richard C.S. Brown United states Agent, for the Cherokee Tribe of Indians came Richard Foreman, (called by some Bark Foreman.) who being duly sworn states, that he is a cherokee, & that he has a white woman for a wife & has several Cherokee Children, that he married, and Lived in the old Cherokee nation East, for many years, was together with his family, Recocgnized [*sic*] as Cherokees by the authorites of the nation, himself & family were all Entitled to the usual priviledges [*sic*], of other Cherokees, and Left the Eastern nation in the month of March

1848, & arrived in the Wester[*n*] Cherokee nation in the month of May last, as well as he Recollects with his family- <u>namely.</u>

1. my self Richard Foreman, (called by some Bark.) over ten years old.
2. Achy Foreman. over ten years old
3. Anthony Foreman, over Ten years old
4. Anna Foreman, over Ten years old
5. Susan Foreman over Ten years old
6. Stephen Foreman over Ten years old
7. Daniel Foreman over Ten years old
8. Catharine Foreman, under Ten years old
9. Robert Foreman under Ten years old
10. Martha Foreman under Ten years old
11. My wife, Rachel Foreman, over Ten years old

The above Enumerated Individuals are my immediate family, who are"
[*end of page*]

[*third page*]

"now under my Charge & Controll; and the following Enumerated persons namely, are, my Daughter & her Children to wit.

12. Jan[*e*] ~~Foreman~~ Hindmon over Ten years old
13. George Wahington Foreman, under Ten years old.
14. Columbus Foreman under Ten years old.

Affiant States all of the above Enumerated, Constituted his family, prior to his leaving the Cherokee nation East, & that he has at his own Individual & Exclusive Expense, Removed the above Enumerated. persons ~~at his own Individual Expense~~ to the Cherokee nation west Affiant States there was no Enrolling agent in the Easter[*n*] Cherokee nation at the time left with his family, in consequence of which he is not prepared to present the Certificate of that officer, that him self & family, to the best of his belief have ~~[*illegible*] of [*illegible*] at any time~~ been Enrolled, for Emigration * ~~West~~ some year since ~~have[?]~~ Removed from the Easte[*rn*] to the

Western * [5] Cherokee nation at the Expense of the United States or the Cherokee people, affiant states that he was Considered at the head of the family of Fourteen, (14) that he Removed to this country- that his Daughter above Enumerated, to gather with his two Children, are a the special Request of the said Jane ~~Foreman~~ Hindman, placed in this my application for ~~[*subsistance?*]~~"
[*end of page*]

[*fourth page*]

"Transportation and Subsistance [*sic*], & that She will file, or cause to be filed here in her affidavit, approbating [sic] this course; affant [*sic*] states that him s[*elf*] & family, are Recognized by the authorities here as Cherokees and have such priviledges [*sic*] as other Cherokees have in this nation, affiant further states has not at any time Received any Commutation of Transportation of Subsistance [*sic*] from the United States, Either in money, or in kind for for [*sic*] the Removal of his said family
further deponant [*sic*] Saith naught

his
Richard X Foreman
mark
{Called by some Bark Foreman}

Sworn to & Subscribed before me this}
day & date above written }
RCS Brown
[*his signature*]
Cherokee Agent"
[*end of page*]

---

[5] Frames no's. 199 (document page two) and 200.(document page three) are duplicates of each other with one small exception. On the second page of the document (frame no. 199) there was a small piece of paper microfilmed over the original paper that says "...but never did remove from the Eastern, to the western Cherokee nation, until now –nor never was...". Astericks in the transcribed document show between what points this piece of paper was laid when microfilmed. Because both pages are duplicates, I have only included a transcription of one.

[*end of document*]

John Dennis Claim, Cherokee Claims for Commutation of Transportation and Subsistence, Treaty of 1835-36. 1845-55. Special File 154, frames 202-204, Special Files of the Office of Indian Affairs; National Archives micropublication M574, roll 32.

[*first page*]

"R305
The United States
To} apt for Subsistance [*sic*] John Dennis
X"
[*end of page*]

[*second page*]

"Cherokee Agency west
Cherok[*ee*] nation

Be it remembered that on this 22nd day of July 1848 before RCS Brown Cherokee Agent personally came John Dennis a white man, with a cherokee family- who being duly sworn states, that [*he*] is a white man, white man, & has a cherokee family that he married a Cherokee Woman by the name of Nancy Vann in the Cherokee nation East & Lived in said nation with said nancy about one year, & about the month of April ~~1822~~ 1832 said affiant Removed from the Eastern nation, to [*illegible*] with his wife & left his son, Westly Dennis, thereabout, two years old, & arrived in the Cherokee nation west, in the month of May ~~[*illegible*]~~ 1832 ~~Remained~~ [*illegible*] as a Citizen of the Westen Cherokee nation ~~[*three words illegible*]~~ &c as [*illegible*] perminantly [*sic*] settled for the purposes of Remaining- affiant states, that some time prior to his leaving the Eastern nation, he had his family & self Enrolled for emigration, with, an Emigrating company, or detachment, under the Charge of Benjamin Curry- he states the reason why he did not bring his son on with him at that time was, he was two [*sic*] small, & was left with some of Relatives, until, some time in the, month of July 1838 he arrived in

Cherokee nation west ~~[illegible]~~ with a company of Emigrants, affiant states that he himself, wife, and son always were Recognized in the old Cherokee nation, as Cherokees, and were entitled to all the priviledges [*sic*] there that other Cherokees were & that they have since in the Western Cherokee nation, been Recognized by the Cherokee authorities, as Cherokees & entitled to priviledges [*sic*] as other Cherokees are, affiant states, that at the time his son came to this country, being a minor under, 21 years of age, & that he is" [*end of page*]

[*third page*]

"under 21 years of age & that he or his father is Entitled to his- years subsistance [*sic*], he further states, neither himself his son, or anyone Else, has ever drawn the subsistance [*sic*] money, herein Claimed Eithe[*r*] in money, or in kind, from the United states, or any of Its' Agents, the Cherokee people, or any other authority whatever, affiant states, that [*illegible*] his papers, prepared, some 18 months since to [*illegible*] by Mr J.M. Bryant, but Mr. Bryant, informes affiant that [*illegible*] [*illegible*], in consequence of which- they were never [*illegible*] on

his
John X Dennis
mark

sworn to & subscribed before me}
this day and date above written }
RCS Brown
[*his signature*]
Cherokee Agent

Cherokee Agency
William Dennis, a whiteman with a Cherokee family being personally presant [*sic*] & hearing the forgoing afft. Read states that the facts as they are stated there in, are true in substance, and in fact
22nd July 1848

his
William **X** Denis [*sic*]
mark

before me

RCS Brown
[*his signature*]
Cherokee Agent".
[*end of page*]
[*end of document*]

Agents Opinions of Claims, Cherokee Claims for Commutation of Transportation and Subsistence, Treaty of 1835-36. 1845-55. Special File 154, frames 205-207, Special Files of the Office of Indian Affairs; National Archives micropublication M574, roll 32.

[*first begins*]

"R305
List of Claims
5 in number
opinion of Agt on <u>Each</u>."
[*end of page*]

[*second page*]

"The following ~~are~~ is a list of Claims for Transportation & subsistance [*sic*] Towit [*sic*]

1st . . . . . John Huffacker

has filed an additional appl. in this case, which, when taken in conncection with Doct. Wm A. Davises affidavit, who is a man of high-standing & [*illegible*] integrity, will sufficiently prove, that applicant is entitled to his claim- (this is one of the 16 sent to this Agency in April last.

2nd . . . . . George Fields.

(This is one of the claims Referred for further Eviedence 25th June 1846.) in addition to the Testimony heretofore, I have procurred from Mr. <u>Fields</u> & herewith Enclose as part of his Evidence. Genl N. Smiths, certificate of Enrollment, to gether with his own additional. afft Explaining &c all of the Evidence taken to gether will Entitle Mr Fields to his claim, unless the Books at your office should, shew [*sic*] a different state of Facts,

3rd . . . . . John Dennis

This is a new application Mr Dennis is a stranger to me, & I submit his claim, with the Evidence, for your own,- consideration,- I have been informed since taking the Testimony of Mr Dennis, & the corobratin [*sic*] Evidence, that both him & Wm Dennis, who coroberates [*sic*] his testimony are both men of Veractiy & that their statements may be relyed [*sic*] on.

4th . . . . . Richard Foreman

This is also a new claim & I am of opinion, is sufficiently well proven up to entitle him to his claim, both Mr Foreman &"
[*end of page*]

[*third page*]

"Brown, his witness are truthful men & Entitled to full Credit on oath

5th . . . . . Sally Bark

This is also a new claim & is doubtless, well proven- up-, & If the Books, of Capt Stephenson, as the disbursing agent whoever [*illegible*] that paid her $100.00 named, in her afft. & to whom she gave up her Enrolling certificate, should not shew [*sic*] a diffrent [*sic*] scale of facts, there can be no dobt [*sic*] of her being Entitled &c. Mrs. Bark, has the Reputation in her neighborhood of being a truthful woman.

Verry [*sic*] Respectfully
Your obt[?] Servt.
RCS Brown
[*his signature*]
Cherokee Agent
1st August 1848"

[*end of page*]
[*end of document*]

Letter Regarding John Ratcliff Claim, Cherokee Claims for Commutation of Transportation and Subsistence, Treaty of 1835-36. 1845-55. Special File 154, frame 208-211, Special Files of the Office of Indian Affairs; National Archives micropublication M574, roll 32.

[*first page*]
[*Note: there appears to be some writing on this document that is very faint and hard to read. That writing has not been included in this transcription. Please reference original document.*]

"Emigr^{t} Cherokee
R. 348
S M Rutherford, [*illegible]*
Oct 20/48
Encl^{d} letter from Ag^{t} Brown covering claim of John Ratcliffe for commu^{n}. transpr & sub &c
See letter to Sup^{t} Rutherford [*illegible*] March '48 & 16 April 1849
claim disallowed-
Rec^{d} 13 Nov. 1848
ak^{d} Nov 14/48"
[*end of page*]

[*second page*]

"Choctaw Agency,
October 20th 1848

Sir:

I have the honor to forward, herewith, a letter from Agent Brown, inclosing the claim of John Ratcliff for transportation and subsistence, with additional proof taken to support the same.

Very respectfully
Your obt Servt.
S.H. [*sic*] Rutherford,
[*his signature*]
Clerk &c

Hon W. Medill
Commr. Ind. Affs.
Washington City."
[*end of page*]

[*third page*]

"R348
To) W. Medill Esqr
commissioner of Indian affairs
Washington City D.C."
[*end of page*]

[*fourth page*]

"Cherokee Agency
October 4th 1848

To Wm Medill Esqr
Commissioner of Indian affairs
Washington City DC

Sir

Enclosed herewith you will find the papers of John Ratcliffe for transportation and Subsistance [*sic*] of Eleven persons (his negroes) with the additional testimony of his Son Charles Ratcliffe, who is represented as being a young man of strict veracity

I am of the opinion that the Claim is Sufficiently proven and should be allowed by the department

Verry [*sic*] Respectfully
Your Obt Servt
RCS Brown
[*his signature*]
Cherokee Agent"

[*end of page*]
[*end of document*]

Letter Regarding David Hilderbrand Claim, Cherokee Claims for Commutation of Transportation and Subsistence, Treaty of 1835-36. 1845-55. Special File 154, frames 212-215, Special Files of the Office of Indian Affairs; National Archives micropublication M574, roll 32.

[*first page*]
[*Note: there appears to be some writing on this document that is very faint and hard to read. That writing has not been included in this transcription. Please reference original document.*]

"Emigration Cherokee
Letter B369.
W Medill
R.C.S. Brown
Jan. 24 '49
In relation to transportation claim of David Hilderbrand, & recommd[g] its allowance
Rec[d] 27 Feb 1849
see letter to Sup[t] Rutherford 16 April '49"
[*end of page*]

[*second page*]

"Cherokee Agency
January 24th 1849

To W. Medill Esq[r]
Commissioner of Indian affairs
W.C. D.C.

Sir

Enclosed I have the honor to send you the Transportation claim of David Hildebrand with his additional Testimony. also the Testimony of Moses Hildebrand, The claim I consider to be a good one. and well proven up, With the Mr. Hildebrands I have no personal acquaintance, but they are men of fair standing in the

Nation, and Moses Hildebrand is Judge of the Tah-le-quah District in the Cherokee Nation,
Col. Thomas F. Taylor, however, who is a highly respectable Cherokee, has certified to the Character of both of them, as you will see, on the back of the Affts- Col. Taylor is well known to the Department as a man of strict veracity, and needs no comment from me.

Very respectfully
Your obt. Servt.
RCS Brown
[*his signature*]
Cherokee Agent"

[*end of page*]

[*third page*]

Letter B.360
W. Medill

Note. I believe I through mistake sent you a letter to the office of the within[*?*] a one or Two days since (without sending the claim)

Civilization [*faint handwriting*]

[*end of page*]

[*fourth page*]

"Cherokee Agency
24th January 1849

To W. Medill Esqr
Commissioner of Indian affairs
W.C. D.C.

Sir Enclosed I have the Honor to send the Transportation claim of David Hildebrand with his additional Testimony, also the Testimony of Moses Hildebrand the claim is considered to be a good one, and well proven up with the Mr Hildebrands, I have no

persoanal acquaintance but they are men of fair standing in the nation, and Moses Hildebrand is judge of the Tah-Le-quah Dist. in the Cherokee naiton.
Col. Thomas F. Taylor however who is a highly respectable Cherokee has certificate to the Character of both of them, as you will see on the Backs of the affts. Col Taylor is well known to the department as a man of Strict veracity & needs no comment from me.

Verry [*sic*] Respectfully
your obt Servt
RCS Brown
[*his signature*]
Cherokee Agent"

[*end of page*]
[*end of document*]

Arch McDaniel Claim, Cherokee Claims for Commutation of Transportation and Subsistence, Treaty of 1835-36. 1845-55. Special File 154, frames 216-221, Special Files of the Office of Indian Affairs; National Archives micropublication M574, roll 32.

[*first page*]
[*Note: there appears to be some writing on this document that is very faint and hard to read. That writing has not been included in this transcription. Please reference original document.*]

"Emigration Cherokee
B448
R.C. S. Brown,
June 15, 1849.
With additional testimony in relation to claim of ~~Alex~~ Arch. M^c^Daniel for commutation &c.
Rec^d^. 11 July 1849"
[*end of page*]

[*second page*]

"Cherokee Nation}
Cherokee Agency}

Personally appeared before Me Richard CS Brown Cherokee Agent Arch McDaniel a Cherokee who being by me first[*?*] duly Sworn States, That he was a citizen of the Cherokee Nation East, that he emigrated under The Treaty of The United States with Cherokee Tribe of Indians of 1835- That he Started from The Cherokee Nation East about The Tenth day of May A.D. 1837- that he did not enroll in The Cherokee Nation prior to his removal or Since. That he removed from The Cherokee Nation East to The Nation West at his own expense, That he Started in company with Saml Mayes[*?*] and Traveled with him to Nashvile [*sic*] Tennessee; from which place he took passage on- Steam Boats to The Nation West- That he is The Son [*of*] William & Torny[*?*] McDanil That his father died in The Nation East prior to the Treaty of 1835 That Torny[*?*] his Mother and his Sister removed in 1834, That he belie[*ve*]s his Mother recei[*v*]ed Commutation and Subs[*istence*] for herself and Daughter- That he has perminently [*sic*] located in the Cherokee Nation West and has Settled in the West with the intention of remaining- That he never was before removed at The expense of The United States or The Cherokee people, or by any other one who was paid therefor That he has never received either transportation or Subsistence for his removal in any manner either by commutation or in kind and That The Sum of fifty Three Dollars and Thirty-Three cents is justly due him for The Same

his
Arch X McDaniel
Mark

Sworn to and Subsc[*r*]ibed before me
15 June AD 1849
R.C.S. Brown
[*his signature*]
Cherokee Agent"
[*end of page*]

[*third page*]

"Cherokee Agency
June 15 1849

Sir

I have Taken an additional Statement from Arch M[c]Daniel in relation to his claim for Transportation and Subsistance [*sic*] accompanying which is The affidavits of Alexander For[*e*]man & John Brewer who are cherokees and men of good Standing for Truth and varacity [*sic*], and I consider Their Statements entitled to credit.

I am verry [*sic*] respectfuly [*sic*]
Your Obt Servt
RCS Brown
[*his signature*]
Cherokee Agent

To W[m] Medill Esq[r]
Com[r] of Indian Affrs
Washington City D.C.

P.S. I further certify that the applicant & Each of the witnisses [*sic*] under stand the English Language & an Interpreter was not necessary.

RCS Brown
[*his signature*]
Cherokee Agent"

[*end of page*]

[*fourth page*]
[*Note: this page is blank with the exception of the number transcribed below.*]

"B448"
[*end of page*]

[*fifth page*]

"Cherokee Nation}
Cherokee Agency}

I Alexander Foreman a citizen of the Cherokee Nation by birth being [*illegible*] duly sworn [*illegible*] State that I am acquainted with Arch M^c^Daniel. That he is a cherokee by birth that he resided and was born in the Cherokee Nation East pri[*o*]r to his removal to the Cherokee Nation West. That he was recognized in the Cherokee Nation East up to the year 1837 as a cit[*e*]zen and entitled to all the rights and of other citizens of the Cherokee Nation, and to all the privleges [*sic*] under the Treaty of 1835 The same Arch M^c^Daniel arrived in the Cherokee Nation West some time in the Spring of 1837- and I believe he emigrated at his own expense- That he is the son [*of*] William M^c^Danel (who died in the Nation East before the removal) and Torny[*?*] M^c^Danel the later removed west in the spring of 1834 in company with myself and that she was enrolled by BF Curry enrolling agent- the said Torny[*?*] removed with her only one[*?*] Daughter- That the said Arch M^c^Daniel has resided in the cherokee nation west permanently since his removal in the spring of 1837 and that he has settled in the nation west with the intention of remaining- That the said Arch M^c^Danel never removed to the Nation West before the Spring of 1837 at the expense of the United States or the Cherokee People or by any one that was paid therefor

Alex Foreman
[*his signature*]

Sworn to and Subscribed before me
This 15th June A.D. 1849
RCS Brown
[*his signature*]
Cherokee Agent

Personally appeared before me John Brewer who is a cit[*i*]zen of the cherokee nation by birth who being first duly sworn states that he is acquainted with Arch M^c^Daniel that he was a cit[*i*]zen of the Cherokee Nation East and that he removed to the cherokee nation west that he was entitled to all the rights of a citzen [*sic*] of"

[*end of page*]

[*sixth page*]

"the Cherokee Nation East as well as to the privileges under the Treaty of 1835- that he has permenetly [*sic*] settled in the Nation west with the intention of remaining. That hes [*sic*] a citzen [*sic*] of the Cherokee Nation West at this time and entitled to all its rights as such

John Brewer
[*his signature*]

Sworn to and Subscribed before me
15th June AD 1849
RCS Brown
[*his signature*]
Cherokee Agent"
[*end of page*]
[*end of document*]

Letter Regarding James Langley, Cherokee Claims for Commutation of Transportation and Subsistence, Treaty of 1835-36. 1845-55. Special File 154, frames 222-223, Special Files of the Office of Indian Affairs; National Archives micropublication M574, roll 32.

[*first page*]
[*Note: there appears to be some writing on this document that is very faint and hard to read. That writing has not been included in this transcription. Please reference original document.*]

"Emigration Cherokee
B490
R.C.S.Brown
16 Augt 1849,
Respecting James Langley's claim for Transpn. & Subsistence &c
Recd 12 Sept 1849"

[*end of page*]

[*second page*]

"Cherokee Agency
16th Augt 1849.

To Brown
Commissioner of Indian
Affairs W.C. D.C.

sir

James Langley a Cherokee has called on me in regard to his transportation & subusistance [*sic*] claim, he states in 1834 ('44) or 1835 (45) he arrived in the Cherokee nation west that he had an Enrolling certificate, from W. Deadrick, Enrolling agent in the eastern nation, Embracing himself, wife & 2 children that shortly after he arrived ~~were[?]~~ in the cherokee nation west, he placed his Enrolling certificate in the hands of Govr Butler the then Agent, who informed him he would Report it to the department & have his money forwarded and since which time, he states he has not had any relyable [*sic*] account of it- I must Request of you Respectfully, to have an Examination made, & [illegible] any papers have Ever been presented to the office, & what if any action has been taken with them, & write to this office

Verry [*sic*] Respectfully
your obt. servt.
RCS Brown
[*his signature*]
Cherokee Agent"

[*end of page*]
[*end of document*]

Luther Crutchfield and Charles Vickery Claim, Cherokee Claims for Commutation of Transportation and Subsistence, Treaty of 1835-36. 1845-55. Special File 154, frames 224-234, Special Files

of the Office of Indian Affairs; National Archives micropublication M574, roll 32.

[*first page*]
[*Note: there appears to be some writing on this document that is very faint and hard to read. That writing has not been included in this transcription. Please reference original document.*]

"Emigration Cherokee
B. 491
Letter
R.C.S. Brown
18 Aug[r]. 1849,
With add[l]. evidence in the cases of Luther Crutchfield & Chas. Vickory who claim for transp[n?] & subst.
Rec[d] 12 Sept 1849."
[*end of page*]

[*second page*]

"Cherokee agency
18th August 1849

To Brown
Commissioner of Indian affairs
Washington City D.C.

sr

I have the honor to send you Enclosed 2 claims for Transporation & Subsistance [*sic*] Towit. 1. For Luther Crutchfield with two additional affidavits, this claim was Returned to this office from the In department a short time since, with the commissioners Remark thus (Suspended) must proof as to his parantage [*sic*]) (meaning I suppose that M[r] Crutchfield should provide[*?*] Evidence as to his parantage [*sic*], which he has done, by his own additional affidavit, & the affidavit of John A. Watie, a Cherokee & United States ~~agent~~ Interpreter, to the Cherokee nation, and a man [*illegible*] respectable standing, I am of opinion that this claim, is fully proven, & should be allowed .

The other is the Claim of Charles Vickory, with his own affft. of Mrs. Black. I consider the claim substancially, & well proven up. unless the words in the Indian department, should shew a differe[*n*]t state of facts, to Exist[*?*],- I am not personally acquainted, with Either M[r] Vickory, Mrs. Black cannot"
[*end of page*]

[*third page*]

"speak of their standing of my own knowledge, but Learn from Relyable [*sic*] persons, that they are good & Worthy citizens, Industrious, Honest, & Truthful, it seems to me that the Claims should be allowed

Verry [*sic*] Respectfully
your obt. servt
RCS Brown
[*his signature*]
Cherokee Agent"

[*end of page*]

[*fourth apge*]

"B491
Luther Crutchfields
Claim for
Transportation
<u>& Subsistence</u>

Suspended.
This claim was suspended by the Com[r] & sent back to the Agent in order that the claimant furnish evidence as to his parentage that the Dept might know if he belonged to Jos. Crutchfields family which, by the head thereof, rec[d] a commutation of trans & sub. in 1837. The additional proof is considered satisfactory [*illegible*] that he was not a son of Jos. Crutchfield- The claim should be allowed.

Oct: 1849

R304
B491
X new Claim."
[*end of page*]

[*fifth page*]

"Cherokee Agency West

Be it known that on this 17th day of July 1848 before me RCS Brown Cherokee Agent, personally came Luther Crutchfield who after being sworn, states that he is a Cherokee Indian, that he was raised, & Resided in the Eastern Cherokee nation, until about 1838. that he was at the hi[*?*]l about 12 years of age, and Removed & Resided in Marion County, in Tennessee, with one Joseph Martin [*could be Marlin*] until, in the year of 1841 & then Lived with one William Woods, in the same County, until in the year 1842 at which time he Removed to Hamblton [*Hamilton*] County Tennessee & lived there with a man by the name of Thomas Wricehain[*?*], until 1844, & then lived with a man by the name of Sterling Condry, until 1846, & then Lived with a man by the name of James Smith, until 1847 & from thence Emigrated by way of Natchez, Mississippi state of [*illegible*] to this country, the Cherokee nation west, where affiant states that he has perminantly [*sic*] settled for the purpose of Remaining, affiant states that was. while in the E[*a*]stern Cherokee nation, & has been since in the Western Cherokee nation, always Recognized by the Cherokee Authorities, as a Cherokee, & allowed such priveledges [*sic*], as other Cherokees were

affiant states that he never was to his knowledge, Enrolled in any attachments company- or family for Emigration of his knowledge, that there was no Enrolling agent, in the Eastern Cherokee nation at the time he left to Enable him to, be [*illegible*] Enrolled.

affiant states that, he Removed himself from the Eastern to the Western Cheorkee nation, at his own, Entire, & Exclusive, Expense, the he never has either directly, or indirectly Rec[d] any Commutation of Transportation, and Subsistence, Either in money, or in kind, from the united states, the Cherokee people or from any other authority, whatsoever therefore prays that his Transportation & subsistence money may be forwarded to him, thro[*u*]gh the" [*end of page*]

[*sixth page*]

"proper Channell affiant states that he arrived in the Cherokee nation West ~~on~~ the month of september last, & Reported himself to Col James McKissick, Cherokee Agent, about the 10th day of January 1848, a short time before his death, which will account for his not making his application-, at an Earlier day than this.

Sworn to & Subscribed } his
before me this day & date } Luther **X** Crutchfield
above written } mark
RCS Brown
[*his signature*]
Cherokee Agent

Cherokee Agency,

Be it known, that on this 17th day of July 1848, before me RCS Brown, Cherokee Agent, personally came Dirt thrower Tyger, a full Blood Cherokee, who being duly sworn through the United States Interpreter, John A. Watie, who, being first duly sworn truly to Interp[*r*]et, states, that he was acquainted with Luther Crutchfield, in the old nation, that was raised in said nation, & is a Cherokee, & that he Removed, & settled perminantly [*sic*], in the Cherokee nation west as he believes perminantly [*sic*], that the said Luther, was Recogniz[ed], ~~moved~~ by the Cherokee Authorities in the [*e*]ast as a Cherokee, & he was Entitled[?] to such priviledges. As other Cherokees were & that has all such priviledges, here as other Cherokees have, & is Regarded by the authorities here as a Cherokee

further deponant [*sic*] saith naught.

Sworn to &Subscribed before me this date above.
RCS Brown his
[*his signature*] Dirtthrower **X** Tyger.

Cherokee Agent. mark"
[*end of page*]

[*seventh page*]

"The United States
To Luther Crutchfield &c

To Transportation $2000
one year's subsistence 33.33 1/3

$53.33 1/3"

[*end of page*]

[*eigth page*]

"B491
Luther Crutchfields additional Testimony
Filed 16th Augt. 1849"
[*end of page*]

[*ninth page*]

"Cherokee Agency

Be it known that on this 16th day of August 1849, personally came Luther Crutchfield a Cherokee who after being duly sworn, makes the following state ment [*sic*] to wit: States that his father was by the name of Edmond Crutchfield (a white man with a Cherokee family) that he his father died when desponant was a small boy, & several years prior to the Treaty of 1845 & 6 [*sic*] he also states that his mother was a full Blood Cherokee named Polly, who after the death of his father was married to a man by the name of Samuel Fowling [*could be Fawling*] who is to gather [*sic*] ~~still living~~ with his mother still living.

Sworn to & Subscribed } his

Before me this date above} Luther X Crutchfield
RCS Brown mark
[*his signature*]
Cherokee Agent."
[*end of page*]

[*tenth page*]

"B491
Luther Crutchfields
Additional Evidence
By
John A. Watie"
[*end of page*]

[*eleventh page*]

"Cherokee Agency.

Be it remembered that on this 16th day of August 1849, personally before me R.C.S. Brown Cherokee Agent came John A. Watie, a Respectable Cheroke[*e*] to me well known, who being duly sworn states, that he is well acquainted with Luther Crutchfield the applicant for Transportation and subsistence, that he knew him in the old Cherokee nation, ~~illegible~~ that he was the son [*of*] Edmon Crutchfield, a white man with a Cherokee family- & that said Edmond Crutchfield died prior to the Cherokee Treaty of 1835-36.

Sworn to & subscribed } John A. Watie
Before me this date above } [*his signature*]
RCS Brown
[*his signature*]
Cherokee Agent"
[*end of page*]
[*end of document*]

Charles Vickery Claim, Cherokee Claims for Commutation of Transportation and Subsistence, Treaty of 1835-36. 1845-55.

Special File 154, frames 235-240, Special Files of the Office of Indian Affairs; National Archives micropublication M574, roll 32.

[*first page*]

"B491
Cha[*r*]les Vicko[r]y

Mary Blacks
Evidence"
[*end of page*]

[*second page*]

"Cherokee Agency.

Be it Remembered that on this 17th day of August 1849, before me RCS Brown Cherokee Agent personally came, Mary Black, a white woman, who after being duly sworn states, that, she was well acquainted with the applicant Charles Vickory a Cherokee, who was, Raised, & Resided for many years in the Eastern Cherokee nation & was Recognized as Cherokees, by the Cherokee,- Authorities, & Entitled to such priveleges [*sic*], as other Cherokees, that, Charles Vickory, to gather [*sic*] with his wife, & three, Cherokee Children, left the Eastern Cherokee nation, in March, 1844 and Removed to the west, & arrived in the western Cherokee nation, in May the same year, & have remained, there perminantly [*sic*] settled, ever since, & have been Recognized as Cherokees by the Cherokee Authorities, here, & have had the usual priveledges [*sic*] of other Cherokees,

affiant states that she believes that the said Charles Vickory, wife, & three, Children were Removed from the East, to the west, at the Enti[*r*]e, & Exclusive, Cost & Expense, of him, the said Charles Vickory, affiant states, that She believes, that the said Vickory, has not at any time, Received any thing from the Goverment [*sic*] of the united states, for the Transportation, and subsistence, of himself, wife & three Children, Either in money, or in kind, nor has he at any time re[cd] any thing, from the Cherokee people for pay, or in part pay, for the same, affiant states, that she lived, a neighbour [*sic*] to

Mr Vickery in the Eastern Cherokee nation, & Removed from there, to the Western Cherokee nation in company with him, & have lived near him & family,="
[*end of page*]

[*third page*]

"ever since he settled in the western Cherokee nation which enables her to have a Covert Knowledge of the manner. in which he Removed from the East. to the west: that neither himself. or any member of his family herein named ever, was Removed from the East, to the west before,- at the Expense of the united states. or of the Cherokees

further deponant saith naught

sworn to & subscribed }
before me this day }
and date above written }

her
Mary X Black
mark

RCS Brown
Cherokee Agent

B491
Charles Vicko[*r*]y

Mary Blacks
Evidence"
[*end of page*]

[*fourth page*]

"B491
Charles Vickory's aft & application for Transportation & subsistence for 5- persons

X"
[*end of page*]

[*fifth page*]

"Cherokee Agency.

Be it Remembered that on this seve[n]th day of August 1849, before me, RCS Brown, Cherokee Agent, personally came Charles Vickory, a Cherokee who being duly sworn states, that he is a cherokee with a white wife; and several Children, he states that he was born and raised in the Cherokee nation East, & that himself & family, were entitled to the usual priveldges [*sic*], there of other Cherokees, & were recognized by the Cherokee Authorities, as such that some time in March 1844 he, to gather [sic] with his wife & three Children, Removed from the Eastern Cherokee nation, to the west, & arrived in the Western Cherokee nation, Some time in the month of May, 1844, & ~~[*illegible*]~~ & perminently [*sic*] settled in, & have remained in the Cherokee nation ever since, affiant states that, he Enrolled himself wife & three Children, with one John Timpson, who he believes was an Enrolling agent at the time, but did not get an Enrolling Certificate, he states that, Removed himself & family, from the East to the west at his Entire & Exclusive, Expensee, that he has ever since, here has, subsisted himself & family, he state, that he never has, Received, any thing Either in money, or in Kind, for either the Transportation, or subsistance [*sic*], of himself & family- or for either of them, from the united states, or their authorities, or from the Cherokee people, but has been at the Entire Expense, of his removal and subsistance [*sic*], that he and his family, were, not attached, to any, company, or detachment whatever, he states that soon after his arrivel [*sic*] here he Reported himself & family to Governor Butler the then Agent & authorized Col. Stan Coaugh[?], who was at the time in this country, to procure his Transportation & subsistance [*sic*]"
[*end of page*]

[*sixth page*]

"for himself, wife, & three Children, ~~to procure[?]~~ & send to him, since which time, he has had no account from Col Stev[*enson?*], although he has written to him on the subject.

Therefore, prays that the Indian department, at washing ton [*sic*] city will make the allowance due to him, for himself, wife, & Three Children, & forward it to the Cherokee Agent in the west, with an order to pay over to him at some early day.

affiant further states that himself and family have since in the west; Enjoyed the usual priveledges [*sic*], of other Cherokees, and been by the Cherokee Authorities, Recognized as Cherokees he states that his father was a whiteman, by the name of Henry Vickory & that he died in 1831- as well as he recollects prior to the Cherokee Treaty of 1835-1836 that his mother was a Cherokee woman, by the name of Charlett who has never inter married, since the death of his father, & still Remains in the Eastern Cherokee nation

further deponant saith naught.

Sworn to and subscribed } Charles Vickery
before me this day and } [*his signature*]
date above written. }
RCS Brown
[*his signature*]
Cherokee Agent"
[*end of page*]
[*end of document*]

Patsey Raper Claim, Cherokee Claims for Commutation of Transportation and Subsistence, Treaty of 1835-36. 1845-55. Special File 154, frames 241-243, Special Files of the Office of Indian Affairs; National Archives micropublication M574, roll 32.

[*first page*]

"Emigration ~~[*illegible*]~~ Cherokee Ag[y]
B494.
~~Letter~~
R.C.S. Brown,
20 Aug[t] 1849.
Invites attention to transp. & subs. claim of Patsey Raper, widow of Andrew Raper, dec[d] &c.

Ag[t.] Bulter had[?] not arrived at date &c"
[*end of page*]

[*second page*]

"Cherokee Agency
20th August 1849

To ... Brown
commissioner of Indian affairs,
Washington City, D.C.

sir

Patsy Raper, a Cherokee, the widow of Andrew, J. Raper, deceased, a Cherokee with her husbands Transportation & subsistance [*sic*] claim. Mrs. Raper assures me that her husband had handed over his Enrolling list to Gov[r] Butler, some short time before he left the office, as Agent, & the Gov[r.] assured him that he would forward it to Washington, as to the Indian department, for payment, she states that her husband died near 4 years since, & that she has not had any account from the Government, Relative to the Claim, & asks me to write this as a letter of Enquiry to the department Trusting that the department will give her such information in regard to the matter or they may be in possion [*sic*] [*'ses' added above this word*] of, Mrs. Raper presents the Copy of a certificate of Enrolling agent, dated 18th Jany. 1844, which Copy, I see has been written by Gov[r] Butler, but it is"
[*end of page*]

[*third page*]

"somewhat Torn & mutilated, so that a part of it has to be guessed at.- I have no doubt but the original is Genuine, & such information as you may feel dis posed [*sic*] to Give her Relative to the Claim, will much oblige the applicant.

Verry [*sic*] Respectfully

Your obt. Servt.
RCS Brown
[*his signature*]
Cherokee Agent

Note: my successor, Mr Butler, has not yet arrived."
[*end of page*]
[*end of document*]

Moses Fields/John Fields Claim, Cherokee Claims for Commutation of Transportation and Subsistence, Treaty of 1835-36. 1845-55. Special File 154, frames 244-245, Special Files of the Office of Indian Affairs; National Archives micropublication M574, roll 32.

[*first page*]
[*Note: there appears to be some writing on this document on the first page that is very faint and hard to read. That writing has not been included in this transcription. Please reference original document.*]

"[*illegible*] Cheorkee ag^{y}
B.536
R.C.S. Brown
[*illegible*] 1849
~~Letter~~
~~[*illegible*]~~
Enquires on application of M. Fields, [*illegible*], in relation to claim of John Fields &
-ag^{t} Butler not arrived at ag^{y} &c.

over

Rec^{d} 27 Nov. 1849.
Civilization.
[*end of page*]

[*second page*]

"Cherokee Agency
1st Novr 1849.

To Orlando Brown Esqr
Commissioner of Indian affairs
Dept. of Interior W.C. D.C.

sir

a few days since I was called on by Moses Fields to know what had become of the application of his Brother John Fields for Transportation and subsistance [*sic*] for himself; wife; 2. sons under Ten years old 2 Daughters under Ten years old & one Daughter over Ten years old & his mother in all nine persons, Mr Fields Tells me, that his brother John Fields, made his application before Govr Butler, when he was Agent & that his brother shortly afterwards died. & that he Moses Fields, is the Administrator of said John Fields, Estate, & that no report has ever been made by the Department ~~so far~~[?] to his Knowledge and now respectfully Requests, that you will at your earliest convenience in form [*sic*] the Agent of what has been the result of his brothers claim.

verry [*sic*] Respectfully
Your obt. Servt.
RCS Brown
[*his signature*]
Cherokee Agent

Note Doct Butler the Cherokee Agent, Recently appointed has not arrived.

2CSB.[?] Cd[?]"

[*end of page*]
[*end of document*]

Nathaniel Peak Claim, Cherokee Claims for Commutation of Transportation and Subsistence, Treaty of 1835-36. 1845-55.

Special File 154, frames 246-248, Special Files of the Office of Indian Affairs; National Archives micropublication M574, roll 32.

[*first page*]

"~~J.J.A.[?]~~ Emigration Cherokee
P.308

Nathaniel Peak
Jany. 23. 1849

Desires money for subsistence, removal and Spoliation [*sic*] &c. under Cherokee treaty- is ready to remove &c.

Recd. Jany. 31. 1849.
ansd. Feby 9/49

civilization
[*end of page*]

[*second page*]

"Tellico Plains Ten Jany 23 1849-

To. W. Medill Esqr
War Department

Your favour of [*illegible*] duly in Said contacts noted As to the fact of my removal I will- state that my Family say my Two Sons and my self were included in the census- And they my two sons removed to the Arkansas at the time of the removal of the Cherokees from Tennessee in the year 1836- and have since resided there I have my self resided in North Carolina and have intended to remove so soon as I could get from the War Department the means for my Removal as I am and always have been ready and willing to remove if I could get the Means as I am desirous to be with my destiny[?] And my object in troubling you at this time is for you to point out to me or provide for me the Means by which I may be able to get the Money that I may put my intentions into effect and

remove to the Indian Count[*r*]y beyond the Mississippi When I am assured it is the wish and intention of the Government I should be- and am thus far on my way from North Carolina which I left some tene [*sic*] months since with no intention of returning there again but to go on from here, when I am living on my friends untile [*sic*] the Goverment [*sic*] shall furnish me the Means to go hence to the Arkansas[.] You will readily ascertain from a refference [*sic*] to the Documents, that I have never received one Dollar from Government for subsistence, for Removal, Spoilations, or in any Monnie and am acutally on my way to the Arkansas in good faith as a good Citizen, and only await"
[*end of page*]

[*third page*]

"some means to acutally procure[*?*] on my way the place of Destination[.] All these facts as I have Notice[*d*] them can be vouched for by the but possible authority on oath if required, And I need not assure you that in these my claims, I submit my case to you and ask your attention in behalf of one who is in every respect a substantial and absolute recipient of that which is asked at your hands[.]

If you my Dear Sir will so far subsene[*?*] my interests by adrising [*sic*] me or facilitating the accomplishment of my objects you will confer a [*illegible*] debt of gratitude on your faithful

Servant-
Nathaniel Peak
[*his signature*]

Be pleased to address me at this place when I extend[*sic*] to remain until I am further addresed [*sic*]

You[*r*] s---t
N. Peak
[*his signature*]"

[*end of page*]
[*end of document*]

Charles Bushyhead Claim, Cherokee Claims for Commutation of Transportation and Subsistence, Treaty of 1835-36. 1845-55. Special File 154, frames 249-252, Special Files of the Office of Indian Affairs; National Archives micropublication M574, roll 32.

[*first page*]

"Emg$^{n.}$ Cherokee
R406
S.M. Rutherford
Jany 15. 1849.
Inc. letter of Ag$^{t.}$ Brown relative to claim of Cha$^{s.}$ Bushyhead-Cherokee

1845 A 1909

Rec^{d} Feby. 7. 1849
Ans^{d} " 7 March

Civilization"
[*end of page*]

[*second page*]

"Choctaw Agenty
January 15. 1849.

Sir,

Inclosed [*sic*] I have the honor to forward a communication from Agent Brown upon the subject of a claim of Charles Bushyhead for transportation and subsistence, alledged to have been placed in the hands of the Cherokee Agent for transmission to the Department in 1844.

Very respectfully
Your obt. servt.
S.M. Rutherford

[*his signature*]
Acting Supt. W.T.

Hon. W. Medill
Commr. Ind. Affs.
Washington City.
[*end of page*]

[third page]

"R. 406.
Agent R.C.S. Brown
Dec 20. 1848"
[*end of page*]

[*fourth page*]

"Cherokee Agency
Decr 20th 1848

To W. Medill Esqr
Commissioner of Indian Affairs
W.C. D.C.

Sir

at the Request of Charles Bushyhead, a Cherokee, I beg leave to make the following enquiry of the Indian department

Mr. Bushyhead called a the office to day to Enquire about his claim for Transportation & subsistance [*sic*], of which I find no trace in the office,- He states that he made out his claim for Transportation & subsistance [*sic*] before Gov. Butler, he believes in the summer of 1844. he is certain that Gov. Butler sent his claim on to the department at the time, for he was liveing [*sic*] with him and acting as Interpreter, that the Gov. assured him the allowance would be made & the money forwarded to him in a short time but states he had not heard a word about this claim since, & I now write to ascertain. If his claim has ever reached the department, in any way- & If so- what, (If any thing,) has been done with it, he is anxious to know whether he is to Get anything or not.

Verry Respectfully
Your obt. servt
RCS Brown
[*his signature*]
Cherokee Agent."

[*end of page*]
[*end of document*]

Moses Fields Claim, Cherokee Claims for Commutation of Transportation and Subsistence, Treaty of 1835-36. 1845-55. Special File 154, frames 253-256, Special Files of the Office of Indian Affairs; National Archives micropublication M574, roll 32.

[*page begins*]

"Emigration Cherokee
R428

S.M. Rutherford, Jany. 31. 1849.

Encl^{g}.letter from agent Brown, with claim of Moses Field, for subsistence &c.

[*two words in faint handwriting are illegible*]

Rec^{d}. 6 March, 1849.
See letter to Sup^{t}. Rutherford 16 April 49"
[*end of page*]

[*second page*]

"Choctaw Agency
January 31st. 1849

Sir:

Herewith enclosed; you will find a letter from Agent Brown, in relation to the claim of Moses Field, a cherokee, for subsistance [*sic*], and, also the affidavit of said Field relative thereto.

Very respectfully
Your obt. Servt
S.M. Rutherford
[*his signature*]
Acting Supt. W.T.

Hon. W. Merill
Commr. Ind Affs
Washington City"
[*end of page*]

[*third page*]

"R428
W. Medill"
[*end of page*]

[*fourth page*]

"Cherokee Agency
January 13th. 1848

sir

Enclosed here with you will find an afft. of Moses Fields, a Respectable Cherokee, you will perceive from his afft. that he Sold his Subsistance [*sic*] claim to Vann who drew, a part of the Subsistance [*sic*] money, & died,- since which time Vanns Admrs. have obtained Judgement, against Fields, for the Resadue [*sic*] of his subsistance [*sic*] Claims,

Consequently so much thereof, or has not been paid heretofore is comeing [*sic*] to Fields.

Respectfully

Your obt. Servt.
RCS Brown
[*his signature*]
Cherokee Agent

W. Medill Esqr
Commissioner of Indian affairs
W.C. D.C."
[*end of page*]
[*end of document*]

Extracts

These documents have been extracted, not transcribed, from the microfilmed originals. The information that has not been included in the extracts are number of family, transportation amount awarded, subsistence amount awarded, and total amount received. You can acquire this information by viewing the microfilmed copy.

Abstract of Payments Made by Philip Minis Under Treaty of 1835, Cherokee Claims for Commutation of Transportation and Subsistence, Treaty of 1835-36. 1845-55. Special File 154, frame 64, Special Files of the Office of Indian Affairs; National Archives micropublication M574, roll 32.

"…Abstract- of payment made by Philip Minis on account of Transportation and year's Subsistence of Cherokees- under the Treaty of 1835…

…Year & Quarter…			…To whom paid…				
				"	"	"	Jacob Nicholson
				"	"	"	Alex^{r} Droomgool
1836.	4th	qr.	Johnson Foreman	"	"	"	Peggy Lassley
1837	1	"	Saml Taylor	"	"	"	Young Puppy
"	"	"	Wm H. Foreman	"	"	"	Archy Downing
"	"	"	Jos. A. Foreman	"	"	"	Es-qua-quat
"	"	"	Stephen Ray	"	"	"	Tec ka wat os ga
"	"	"	Joseph Rogers	"	"	"	Charles Moore
"	"	"	Jacob West	"	"	"	Ailsy Downing
"	"	"	John W. West	"	"	"	Long Shell Turtle
"	"	"	John Brewer	"	"	"	Black bird
"	"	"	Th-nu-wah	"	"	"	Big Milk
"	"	"	Ja^{s} J. Trott	"	"	"	Ooliesanl
"	"	"	Josh: Kirkpatrick	"	"	"	Mary Ann Howel
"	"	"	Thos F. Taylor	"	"	"	Andrew Ross
"	"	"	Saml L. Ballard	"	"	"	Susan J. Harlin…"

Abstract of Payments Made by Philip Minis Under Treaty of 1835, Cherokee Claims for Commutation of Transportation and Subsistence, Treaty of 1835-36. 1845-55. Special File 154, frame 65, Special Files of the Office of Indian Affairs; National Archives micropublication M574, roll 32.

"…Abstract- of payment made by Philip Minis on account of Transportation and year's Subsistence of Cherokees- under the Treaty of 1835…

…Year & Quarter…			…To whom paid…				
				"	"	"	Joshua Buffington
				"	"	"	David Bell
"	"	"	Thos Brewer	"	"	"	Nitts
"	"	"	Tomorrow	"	"	"	John Hawkins
"	"	"	Bear Meat	"	"	"	Samuel M Caman
"	"	"	Killer Moore	"	"	"	Isaac E. Nicholson
"	"	"	Ground Mole	"	"	"	Alleca Swimmer
"	"	"	Culstea Teyolee[?]	"	"	"	Levi B. Jones
"	"	"	Jenny Scon-ah-ta-hee	"	"	"	James A. Thompson
"	"	"	Big Coon	"	"	"	Johnson Thompson
"	"	"	Joseph Scunteah	"	"	"	John Williams
"	"	"	Archy Rowe			"	Johnson Fields- Son of
"	"	"	Perry A Spaniard				Turtle Fields
"	"	"	Robert Sanders	"	"	"	Major Ridge
"	"	"	Edward Graves	"	"	"	William Rogers
"	"	"	James A.D. Brown Jr.	"	"	"	John Boston
"	"	"	Olly Lassley	"	"	"	Joseph Crutchfield
"	"	"	Richard Scott	"	"	"	Johnson Fields…"

Abstract of Payments Made by Philip Minis Under Treaty of 1835, Cherokee Claims for Commutation of Transportation and Subsistence, Treaty of 1835-36. 1845-55. Special File 154, frame 66, Special Files of the Office of Indian Affairs; National Archives micropublication M574, roll 32.

"…Abstract- of payment made by Philip Minis on account of Transportation and year's Subsistence of Cherokees- under the Treaty of 1835…

…Year & Quarter…			…To whom paid…
"	"	"	William Lassley
"	"	"	Black Fox
"	"	"	Cat Fields
"	"	"	Turtle Fields
"	"	"	Ete connah
"	"	"	Leonard Hicks
"	"	"	G.W. Adair
"	"	"	William S. Hicks
"	"	"	David Watie
"	"	"	James Fields
"	"	"	John Elliot
"	"	"	Lovely Rogers
"	"	"	Sally Rain crow
"	"	"	James Matear
"	"	"	John Fields Sr.
"	"	"	Calvin Wolf
"	"	"	Sarah Pig
"	"	"	Danl McCoy
"	"	"	Archey Fields
"	"	"	John Fields Jr
"	"	"	Wiley G. Thornton
"	"	"	David Vann
"	"	"	John Martin
"	"	"	Joseph M. Lynch
"	"	"	Alexander McCoy
"	"	"	Benj^{m} F. Thompson
"	"	"	William Conner
"	"	"	John R. Adair
"	"	"	John T. Adair
"	"	"	William Dennis
"	"	"	Samuel Mayes
"	"	"	Jacob Bushyhead
"	"	"	Elijah Moore
"	"	"	B.F Adair
"	"	"	W^{m} McBride…"

Abstract of Payments Made by Philip Minis Under Treaty of 1835, Cherokee Claims for Commutation of Transportation and Subsistence, Treaty of 1835-36. 1845-55. Special File 154, frame 67, Special Files of the Office of Indian Affairs; National Archives micropublication M574, roll 32.

"…Abstract- of payment made by Philip Minis on account of Transportation and year's Subsistence of Cherokees- under the Treaty of 1835…

…Year & Quarter…			…To whom paid…
"	"	"	Henry Seabolt
"	"	"	John Seabolt
"	"	"	Jonathan & Maria Mulky
"	"	"	John Gunter
"	"	"	Thos Carey
"	"	"	Nelson Harlin
"	"	"	Reuben Tate
"	"	"	William Turner
"	"	"	William Poulston
"	"	"	Larkin Beavert
"	"	"	War-yar-ne-ta
"	"	"	Benjamin Merrill
"	"	"	Alexander Gilbreath

"	"	"	Isaac Spring[*s*]ton
"	"	"	Richard Taylor
"	"	"	Alesander Brown
"	"	"	Peter Barber
"	"	"	Tail
"	"	"	James Davis
"	"	"	James Wilkinson
"	"	"	Jenny Bark
"	"	"	Edward Bark
"	"	"	Swelled Belly
"	"	"	Archilla Smith
"	"	"	Jos. B. Byrd
"	"	"	John Ratliff
"	"	"	Lowry Williams
"	"	"	Captain Baldridge
"	"	"	Robert Brown…"

Abstract of Payments Made by J.P. Simonton Under Treaty of 1835, Cherokee Claims for Commutation of Transportation and Subsistence, Treaty of 1835-36. 1845-55. Special File 154, frame 68, Special Files of the Office of Indian Affairs; National Archives micropublication M574, roll 32.

"...Abstract of payments made by J.P. Simonton- on account of transportation and year's Subsistence of Cherokees- under the treaty of 1835...

...Year & Quarter...			...To whom paid...
1837	2[d]	qr.	Richard Keys
"	"	"	John R. Nicholson
"	"	"	Charles F. Foreman
"	"	"	William A. Davis
"	"	"	Stand Watie
"	"	"	Jay Hicks
"	"	"	Rider Fields
"	"	"	William Beamer
"	4	"	Elias Boudinot
"	"	"	Calvin Jones
"	"	"	G.W. Paschal
"	"	"	David Carter

...Rec[d] in 1835- for Sub[ce] \$200- & for transportation \$270-
See no 6. abstract transportation- 4. q. 1837- Simonton no. 1560
2 auditor's- off-..."

Abstract of Payments Made by Jno. C. Reynolds Under Treaty of 1835, Cherokee Claims for Commutation of Transportation and Subsistence, Treaty of 1835-36. 1845-55. Special File 154, frame 69, Special Files of the Office of Indian Affairs; National Archives micropublication M574, roll 32.

"…Abstract of payments made by Jn° C. Reynolds- on account of Transportation and years subsistence- Cherokee treaty of 1835…

…Year & Quarter…			…To whom paid…
1837	2.	q.	David Wilcoxen
"	"	"	Joseph Cookson
"	"	"	Jesse McLain
"	3.	q.	Anne Seabolt
"	"	"	Samuel Martin
"	"	"	Noah Lillard
"	"	"	Wm S. Richardson
"	"	"	Andrew Sanders
"	"	"	Elizabeth Candy
"	"	"	Thomas Meigs
"	"	"	Thompson Sanders
"	"	"	Daniel B. Hopkins
"	"	"	George Candy
"	"	"	Elizabeth Pettet

"	"	"	Thomas Bigby
"	"	"	Flemuel Childers
"	"	"	Eli Palmer
"	"	"	Lemuel Childers
"	"	"	James C. McNair
"	"	"	Sarah Hicks
"	"	"	Wm S. Rodgers
"	"	"	Andrew Adair
"	"	"	George Miller
"	"	"	James Landrum
"	"	"	Samuel Thomas
"	"	"	Leaf
"	"	"	Akee- or Hanah Light toln[?]
"	"	"	John Huss
"	"	"	Teesy Guess…"

ents Made by Jno. C. Reynolds Under Treaty of 1835, Cherokee Claims for Commutati Treaty of 1835-36. 1845-55. Special File 154, frame 70, Special Files of the Office of In blication M574, roll 32.

yments made by Jn° C. Reynolds- on account of Transportation and years subsistence- Ch

..	...To whom paid...				
		"	"	"	R
qr.	James Mankiller	"	"	"	Jc
"	George Sanders	"	"	"	R
"	Sinews	"	"	"	M
"	Night Killer	"	"	"	G
"	Kartos or Bread	"	"	"	W
"	Pheasant	"	"	"	E
"	John Beamer	"	"	"	G
"	A-ha-sa-tees-ka			paid by	
"	Sar-ke-ah McCoy	1838	2.	qr.	E
"	Jumper	1838	2.	qr.	A
"	Lucinda Hicks				
"	Joseph Spears				
"	Nancy Too ke ah	+ Rob Brown her nephew }			
"	John A. Goddard				
"	+ Peggy Mink	(x) mother of Robert Brown }"			
"	(x) Susannah	*[end of page]*			

Abstract of Payments Made by Joel Crittenden Under Treaty of 1835, Cherokee Claims for Commutation of Transportation and Subsistence, Treaty of 1835-36. 1845-55. Special File 154, frame 71, Special Files of the Office of Indian Affairs; National Archives micropublication M574, roll 32.

"…Abstract of payments made by Joel Crittenden- continued…

...Year & Quarter…			…To whom paid…
1838	4.	qr.	James C. Price
"	"	"	Alexander Raper
"	"	"	Reese Mitchell
"	"	"	Stephen P. Hilderbrand
"	"	"	Rich[d] Fields- for transportation of his brother J.M. Fields
"	"	"	Alece
"	"	"	Path Killer
"	"	"	Henry Nave
"	"	"	Nancy Reed
"	"	"	Nelly Martin
"	"	"	W[m] A. Coleman
"	"	"	George Whitfield
"	"	"	John Catron
"	"	"	Johnson Thompson
"	"	"	John Langley
"	"	"	Jesse Morris
"	"	"	Sarah Sanders
"	"	"	Celia Paris
"	"	"	Ezekiel Fields
"	"	"	John Fields
"	"	"	John Brown
"	"	"	John Wickett
"	"	"	[*illegible*][6] Jackson Mellun
"	"	"	Alfred Garett
"	"	"	Benjamin Dougherty
"	"	"	Mary Barnhill
"	"	"	David Shaw…"

[6] This word has been smeared on the page.

Abstract of Payments Made by Joel Crittenden Under Treaty of 1835, Cherokee Claims for Commutation of Transportation and Subsistence, Treaty of 1835-36. 1845-55. Special File 154, frame 72, Special Files of the Office of Indian Affairs; National Archives micropublication M574, roll 32.

"Abstract of payments made by Joel Crittenden continued-

...Year & Quarter...			...To whom paid...
1839	1	qr	Emily S. Walker
"	"	"	Calvin S. Adair
"	"	"	Abijah Akins
"	"	"	John Tidwell
"	"	"	Christiana Martin
"	"	"	Felix Arthur
"	"	"	George Welch
"	"	"	Charles Duncan
"	"	"	Alfred Scudder
"	"	"	Alfred H. Hudson
"	"	"	Lewis Blackburn
"	"	"	Joseph Vann
"	"	"	Andrew Taylor..."

Abstract of Payments Made by Joel Crittenden Under Treaty of 1835, Cherokee Claims for Commutation of Transportation and Subsistence, Treaty of 1835-36. 1845-55. Special File 154, frame 73, Special Files of the Office of Indian Affairs; National Archives micropublication M574, roll 32.

"Abstract of payments made by Joel Crittenden on account of Transportation and year's Subsistence of Cherokees- under the treaty of 1835.-

...Year & Quarter...			...To whom paid...				
1837	4	qr:	Ellis Beck	"	"	"	Mary Buffington
"	"	"	Jeffrey Beck	"	"	"	Ruth
"	"	"	Joseph Beck	"	"	"	Neely McDaniel
"	"	"	Hiram Landrum	"	"	"	Thunder
"	"	"	Polly Downing & Ary	"	"	"	Robt B. Daniel
			Richardson	"	"	"	Robt Berry's heirs
"	"	"	Ailsey	"	"	"	George Butler
"	"	"	Aaron Downing	"	"	"	John Toney
"	"	"	George Fields. Hamilton	"	"	"	Woman Killer
			Co. Tenn:	"	"	"	George Hughes
"	"	"	Rhoda Fields	"	"	"	Sally Hughes
"	"	"	Mary Ann Harlin	"	"	"	Nancy Graves
"	"	"	Surry Eaton	"	"	"	Ke-u-kah, tu kee[?]
"	"	"	Joshua Roach	"	"	"	Tu, nah, na tlah
"	"	"	Mary Daniel	"	"	"	Stephen Graves
"	"	"	Saml K. Wear	"	"	"	Cross Eyes Watt…"

Abstract of Payments Made by Joel Crittenden Under Treaty of 1835, Cherokee Claims for Commutation of Transportation and Subsistence, Treaty of 1835-36. 1845-55. Special File 154, frame 74, Special Files of the Office of Indian Affairs; National Archives micropublication M574, roll 32.

"Abstract of payments made by Joel Crittenden- continued

...Year & Quarter...			...To whom paid...				
				"	"	"	Chew-ee
				"	"	"	James McCracken
1837	4th	qr.	Thomas Boot	"	"	"	Catherine Wafford
"	"	"	Pheasant- of Kid Hill	"	"	"	Archibald Spears
"	"	"	E George	"	"	"	Dumb-Boy
"	"	"	Wiley Butler	"	"	"	Robin
"	"	"	E-yah-cha-lah	"	"	"	Musk Rat
"	"	"	Horn	"	"	"	Dragging Canoe
"	"	"	Su-wa-ka	"	"	"	Sally
"	"	"	Tre-cah-hoo	"	"	"	Mark Tyger
"	"	"	Tlah-cah	"	"	"	Allen Ross
"	"	"	Richard Sanders	"	"	"	Bull Frog
"	"	"	Peggy Sanders	"	"	"	Wallee, or Polly
"	"	"	Nicholas Sanders	"	"	"	Joseph Crittenden
"	"	"	Peter	"	"	"	Fennel Morgan
"	"	"	Wy-a-lu-ka	"	"	"	Te-sa-es ky
"	"	"	Chick-oo wee	"	"	"	Saml Nellams..."

Abstract of Payments Made by Joel Crittenden Under Treaty of 1835, Cherokee Claims for Commutation of Transportation and Subsistence, Treaty of 1835-36. 1845-55. Special File 154, frame 75, Special Files of the Office of Indian Affairs; National Archives micropublication M574, roll 32.

"Abstract- continued-

...Year & Quarter...			...To whom paid...				
1837	4th	qr	Fishing Hawk	"	"	"	Rich[d] Fields
"	"	"	Jackson Mankiller	"	"	"	William Blyth- Jr:
"	"	"	Nancy	"	"	"	George Fields
"	"	"	John Brown Jr:	"	"	"	John R. Blyth
"	"	"	Rob[t] B. Vann	"	"	"	Moses Fields
"	"	"	Martin D. Cheek	"	"	"	Ira Gothard
1838	1	qr	Charles Stofle	"	"	"	Ellis B. Towers
"	"	"	Eldridge Vaughn	"	"	"	Richard Blackburn
"	"	"	George Dryhead	"	"	"	Jos: B M[c]Laughlin
"	"	"	Smoke Glass	"	"	"	Nancy
"	"	"	James E. Fields	"	"	"	Willis Fields
"	"	"	Charlotte	"	"	"	M. M. Schrimsher
"	"	"	Ezekiel Byer	"	"	"	David Cunsend
"	"	"	James Vann	"	"	"	Allen Ratley
"	"	"	William Blyth- Sen.	"	"	"	J.C. Towers..."

Abstract of Payments Made by Joel Crittenden Under Treaty of 1835, Cherokee Claims for Commutation of Transportation and Subsistence, Treaty of 1835-36. 1845-55. Special File 154, frame 76, Special Files of the Office of Indian Affairs; National Archives micropublication M574, roll 32.

"Abstract of payments made by Joel Crittenden-continued.

...Year & Quarter...			...To whom paid...				
1838	2	qr..	George M. Waters	"	"	"	Brice Martin
"	"	"	William Harris	"	"	"	David Miller
"	"	"	Rance Bird Harris	"	"	"	Charles Vickery
"	"	"	Charles Harris	"	"	"	Samuel Bennet
"	"	"	John Rogers	"	"	"	Jesse Eldridge
"	"	"	Robert Rogers	"	"	"	Charlotte Vickery
"	"	"	Joseph B. Collins	"	"	"	Martin Branham
"	"	"	Nancy Daniel	"	"	"	David M. Harlin
"	"	"	John R. Daniel	"	"	"	Lazarus Gatlin
"	"	"	William Martin	"	"	"	Jane M^c^Pherson
"	"	"	Dick Boggs	"	"	"	James Langley
"	"	"	Jefferson Dougherty	"	"	"	Nancy Hicks
"	"	"	Susannah Guerichess[?]	"	"	"	Samuel Terrel
"	"	"	James Kell	"	"	"	Josephus Richards
"	"	"	Edmund Duncan	"	"	"	Richard Newland
"	"	"	Nancy Spears	"	"	"	Delelah A. M^c^Nair..."

Abstract of Payments Made by Joel Crittenden Under Treaty of 1835, Cherokee Claims for Commutation of Transportation and Subsistence, Treaty of 1835-36. 1845-55. Special File 154, frame 77, Special Files of the Office of Indian Affairs; National Archives micropublication M574, roll 32.

"Abstract of payments made by Joel Crittenden-continued.

...Year & Quarter...			...To whom paid...				
1838	2	qr	Ezekiel Ragsdale	"	3	qr.	Chon-a-you-kah
"	"	"	Benjamin Downing	"	"	"	Che a non-nah Boggs
"	"	"	J.M. Davis	"	"	"	John Riley
"	"	"	Henry H. Sutton	"	"	"	William Bean
"	"	"	Catharine Vaught	"	"	"	D.W. Ivy
"	"	"	Lewis Griffin	"	"	"	William Merrill
"	"	"	John Baldridge	"	"	"	Samuel Canby
"	"	"	James Spencer	"	"	"	Rebeckah Goinsmit[?]
"	"	"	John Baldridge	"	"	"	Gideon Coats
"	"	"	John Dougherty	"	"	"	James Lasley
"	"	"	Edward Wicked	"	"	"	Nancy Mellon
"	"	"	James Leaf	"	"	"	Daniel A. Pardue
"	"	"	Crying Snake	"	"	"	Ailsey Eldridge
"	"	"	Rachel M[c]Daniel	"	"	"	David Kell
"	"	"	Dick Cary	"	"	"	John M[c]Cullough..."
"	"	"	Robert Lovett				

Abstract of Payments Made by Joel Crittenden Under Treaty of 1835, Cherokee Claims for Commutation of Transportation and Subsistence, Treaty of 1835-36. 1845-55. Special File 154, frame 78, Special Files of the Office of Indian Affairs; National Archives micropublication M574, roll 32.

"Abstract of payments made by Joel Crittenden-continued.

...Year & Quarter...			...To whom paid...				
1838	4th	qr	Gideon F. Norris	"	"	"	Charles Butler
"	"	"	David Taylor	"	"	"	Benjamin Bracket
"	"	"	Hawk	"	"	"	Mijamin Bracket
"	"	"	Dianna Diver	"	"	"	Malachi Paris
"	"	"	Hunter Langley	"	"	"	Lock[?] L. Langley
"	"	"	Sally Bark	"	"	"	Caleb Starr
"	"	"	John S. Marsh	"	"	"	A.J. Miller
"	"	"	Adam Seabolt	"	"	"	John- of Chickamauga
"	"	"	Lydda	"	"	"	Sunday Woodward
"	"	"	Jinny Pig	"	"	"	Red Bird Woodward
"	"	"	Thomas Wolf	"	"	"	John Drew
"	"	"	Jonathan England	"	"	"	Charles Thompson
"	"	"	Richd Fields	"	"	"	Saml W. Bell
"	"	"	Hugh Henry	"	"	"	Carrington W. Hicks
"	"	"	Omy Utley	"	"	"	John Kell
"	"	"	Alice Buffington	"	"	"	Isabella Hicks..."
"	"	"	James Martin				

Abstract of Payments Made by M.W. Bateman Under Treaty of 1835, Cherokee Claims for Commutation of Transportation and Subsistence, Treaty of 1835-36. 1845-55. Special File 154, frame 79, Special Files of the Office of Indian Affairs; National Archives micropublication M574, roll 32.

"Abstract of payments made by M.W. Bateman for transportation- &c- of Cherokees-

...Year & Quarter...			...To whom paid...
1835	1	q.	Felix W. Riley
"	"	"	George Harlin
"	"	"	Tho[s] J & Eliza Jordan
"	"	"	Joshua Roach
"	"	"	Silas Chote
"	"	"	Joseph S. Falling
"	"	"	Sanders Chote
"	"	"	Henry & Sally Quinton
"	"	"	George Bearmeat
"	"	"	Reader Moore
"	"	"	Luther Moore
"	"	"	Ezekiel B. M[c]Laughlin
"	"	"	Maria & David M[c]Laughlin
"	"	"	James & Elizabeth Hendricks
"	"	"	John L. M[c]Coy
"	"	"	Dav[??] Burg[???][7]..."

[7] The last part of the surname was barely legible. Please reference original.

Abstract of Payments Made by John Vanhorn Under Treaty of 1835, Cherokee Claims for Commutation of Transportation and Subsistence, Treaty of 1835-36. 1845-55. Special File 154, frame 80, Special Files of the Office of Indian Affairs; National Archives micropublication M574, roll 32.

"Abstract of payments made by J. Vanhorn- for transportation and Subsistence of Cherokees.

...Year & Quarter...			...To whom paid...				
1836	4	q	Sally Stuart	"	"	"	Dianna Woodcock
"	"	"	Giles M^c^Nulty	"	"	"	Chenab-bee
1837	2	q	Elizabeth Thompson	"	"	"	Tes-a-tus-kee
"	"	"	Richard Chuck	"	"	"	Nanny Harris
"	"	"	Justice Fields	"	"	"	Nelly
"	"	"	Watty Squirrel	"	"	"	Stephen Harris
"	"	"	P.H. Nix	"	"	"	Stand
"	"	"	Bread Cutter	"	"	"	Danl Mills
"	"	"	Long Shell Scraper	"	"	"	Ave Vann
"	"	"	Sour Mush	"	"	"	Alexander Scraper
"	"	"	Culstiah	"	"	"	Moses Harris
"	"	"	Te-ki-is-kee	"	"	"	Preacher
"	"	"	George Downing	"	"	"	Buzzard
"	"	"	Issurs[?]	"	"	"	Scontiah
"	"	"	Henry Clay	"	"	"	Culculoskee
"	"	"	Poor Bear	1835	2	qr.	David Burgess..."

Abstract of Payments Made by John Vanhorn Under Treaty of 1835, Cherokee Claims for Commutation of Transportation and Subsistence, Treaty of 1835-36. 1845-55. Special File 154, frame 81, Special Files of the Office of Indian Affairs; National Archives micropublication M574, roll 32.

"Abstract of payments made by John Vanhorn continued

...Year & Quarter...			...To whom paid...				
1837	2	qr	Charles Tracker	"	3	qr.	William E. Lacy
"	"	"	Nancy Walker	"	"	"	John M^c^Culloch
"	"	"	Alexander Downing	"	"	"	James Childers
"	"	"	Peggy Scontiah	"	"	"	James Hendricks
"	"	"	Spring Frog	"	"	"	Che-neh or Watee Dog
"	"	"	Standing Man	"	4	qr.	Achilla Smith
"	"	"	David A. Reese	"	"	"	Clem^t^ V. M^c^Nair
"	"	"	Polly Wilson	"	"	"	Wm S. Rogers
"	"	"	David Griffin	"	"	"	Andrew Sanders
"	"	"	Ned Five Killer	"	"	"	Jesse M^c^Lain
"	"	"	Jane Smith	"	"	"	Johnson Foreman
"	"	"	Wattah	"	"	"	James V. M^c^Nair
"	"	"	Susan Man Killer	"	"	"	Flemuel Childers
"	"	"	Robert M^c^Teas	"	"	"	Andrew Adair
"	"	"	Lawena	"	"	"	George Miller
"	"	"	John L. M^c^Coy	"	"	"	Mary Miller..."

Abstract of Payments Made by John Vanhorn Under Treaty of 1835, Cherokee Claims for Commutation of Transportation and Subsistence, Treaty of 1835-36. 1845-55. Special File 154, frame 82, Special Files of the Office of Indian Affairs; National Archives micropublication M574, roll 32.

"Abstract of payments made by J. Vanhorn- continued-

...Year & Quarter...			...To whom paid...				
1837	4	qr.	George Candy	"	"	"	Nancy Bigbear
"	"	"	Noah Lillard	"	"	"	Rattling Gourd Waters
"	"	"	James M^c^Cracken	"	"	"	Charity waters
"	"	"	Elizabeth Candy	"	"	"	Betsy Sutton
"	"	"	Charles Griffin	"	"	"	Rachel Perdue
"	"	'	Reader Moore	"	"	"	Nancy Dry forehead
"	"	"	Luther Moore	"	"	"	Alen Mush
"	"	"	Rain Frog	"	"	"	Sally Fish
"	"	"	David Downing	"	"	"	Maria Drowning bear
"	"	"	Pheasant	"	"	"	Katy M^c^Pherson
"	"	"	Lucinda Vann	"	"	"	George Waters
"	"	"	Culsowee	"	"	"	Jack Culsowe
"	"	"	Contah ke	"	"	"	Lucy Sweet Water
"	"	"	Charlotte Cordery	"	"	"	Nancy
"	"	"	Jane Beaver	"	"	"	John A. Goddard..."
"	"	"	Dew				
"	"	"	Dreadful Waters				

Abstract of Payments Made by John Vanhorn Under Treaty of 1835, Cherokee Claims for Commutation of Transportation and Subsistence, Treaty of 1835-36. 1845-55. Special File 154, frame 83, Special Files of the Office of Indian Affairs; National Archives micropublication M574, roll 32.

"Abstract of payments made by J. Vanhorn- continued.

...Year & Quarter...			...To whom paid...
1837	4	qr.	Jane Goddard
"	"	"	Water Lizzard
"	"	"	Ti es ke
"	"	"	Chickaleska, or Chu lah lu ky
"	"	"	David Timpson
"	"	"	Inkstand
"	"	"	Betsey Cade & Daughter Maria..."

Abstract of Payments Made by John Vanhorn Under Treaty of 1835, Cherokee Claims for Commutation of Transportation and Subsistence, Treaty of 1835-36. 1845-55. Special File 154, frame 84, Special Files of the Office of Indian Affairs; National Archives micropublication M574, roll 32.

"Abstract of payments made by J. Vanhorn- continued.

...Year & Quarter...			...To whom paid...				
1838	1	qr.	Thomas Soo-a-killer	"	"	"	John Dear head
"	"	"	Charles Vann	"	"	"	Cho-u-ayon-kah
"	"	"	David Gage	"	"	"	Johnson Hughes
"	"	"	Joshua Buffington & for	"	"	"	Sarah Hicks
			his child	"	"	"	James Taylor or Jas. V.
"	"	"	Joseph M. Lynch- do-do				Taylor
"	"	"	John Ridge	"	"	"	John A. Wayne
"	"	"	Hah-lin-war-tas-kee	"	"	"	Jesse Halfbreed
"	"	"	Alfred Ellidge	"	"	"	Tan-chu-la-nah or Clem
"	"	"	Catherine Wofford				Foster
"	"	"	Chick o les kee	"	"	"	Crying Wolf
"	"	"	William Pettit	"	"	"	Wattie (a woman)
"	"	"	Yonah- or Bear	"	"	"	Jack Six Killer
"	"	"	James Dear head	"	"	"	Sampson Pryor
"	"	"	Ande- including Nancy	"	"	"	Elijah Burs
			Neckskin	"	"	"	Elizabeth Shoe boots
"	"	"	Thomas Meigs	"	"	"	Crawler Wicked
"	"	"	Barney Hughs	"	"	"	Oo-la-nes-tah…"

Abstract of Payments Made by John Vanhorn Under Treaty of 1835, Cherokee Claims for Commutation of Transportation and Subsistence, Treaty of 1835-36. 1845-55. Special File 154, frame 85, Special Files of the Office of Indian Affairs; National Archives micropublication M574, roll 32.

"Abstract of payments made by J. Vanhorn- continued.

...Year & Quarter...			...To whom paid...				
1838	1	qr.	Anne Seabolt	"	"	"	Nicko Jack
"	"	"	Ground Hog	"	"	"	E-chu-ka
"	"	"	Jesse Murphy or Big nee	"	"	"	Corn Tassel
			Jesse	"	"	"	Thomas Bigby
"	"	"	Lemuel Wilson	"	"	"	Charles Vann
"	"	"	Tuck-se-wah-[*?*] or	"	"	"	Isaac Walker
			Terrapin Striker	"	"	"	David Gage
"	"	"	Watty- included is	"	"	"	Peter Hogar[*?*]
			Nancy Big bear's family	"	"	"	Six killer
"	"	"	Richard Timberlake	"	"	"	Elizabeth Pettis
"	"	"	Joseph Starr	"	"	"	Necey McDaniel
"	"	"	Thomas Starr	"	"	"	Stooping Tree- Mush
"	"	"	Charles Reese	"	"	"	Big Mush
"	"	"	Eliza or Widow Maw	"	"	"	Katy Cade
"	"	"	James Starr	"	"	"	John Fish
"	"	"	Charles Timberlake	"	"	"	Robert Waters
"	"	"	A-tah-hee	"	"	"	July
"	"	"	Hilliam [*sic*] Grimmet	"	"	"	Martha C. Mosely..."

Abstract of Payments Made by John Vanhorn Under Treaty of 1835, Cherokee Claims for Commutation of Transportation and Subsistence, Treaty of 1835-36. 1845-55. Special File 154, frame 86, Special Files of the Office of Indian Affairs; National Archives micropublication M574, roll 32.

"Abstract of payments made by J. Vanhorn- continued-

...Year & Quarter...			...To whom paid...
1838	1	q.	George Fields
"	"	"	Thompson Sanders
"	"	"	William S. Richardson
"	"	"	Daniel B. Hopkins
"	"	"	Te-sa-Guess
"	"	"	George Saunders
"	"	"	Chu-quel-kah
"	"	"	James Hughes
"	"	"	Joshua Buffington, one child
"	"	"	Joshua Buffington- Guardian of R. Berry'[*s*] heirs
"	"	"	Joseph M. Lynch- one child
"	"	"	Jim Cow
"	"	"	Hiram Landrum
"	"	"	A-hee-a-tes-ka
"	"	"	Pheasant
"	"	"	Lucy Sweetwater
"	"	"	Lemuel Childress
"	"	"	Eli Palmer
"	"	"	Ways kee
"	"	"	Jeffry Beck
"	"	"	Ellis Beck
"	"	"	Surry Eaton
"	"	"	Polly Downing
"	"	"	Ary Richards
"	"	"	Joseph Beck
"	"	"	Pheasant
"	"	"	E. George
"	"	"	Wiley Butler
"	"	"	Thomas Boots
"	"	"	Ki-u-kah-tee-hee
"	"	"	Night Killer..."

Abstract of Payments Made by John Vanhorn Under Treaty of 1835, Cherokee Claims for Commutation of Transportation and Subsistence, Treaty of 1835-36. 1845-55. Special File 154, frame 87, Special Files of the Office of Indian Affairs; National Archives micropublication M574, roll 32.

"Abstract of payments made by John Vanhorn- continued-

...Year & Quarter...			...To whom paid...
1838	1	qr.	Cah-tos- or Bread
"	"	"	Sinews
"	"	"	Sar-kee-he- or M:Coy
"	"	"	Thomas McCoy
"	"	"	Widow- Big Dollars
"	"	"	Akee or Hannah Light Carrie[*s?*]
"	"	"	John Huss
"	"	"	Nelly
"	"	"	Jacob Seabold
"	"	"	Stephen Graves
"	"	"	Jackson Mankiller
"	"	"	Elizabeth Justice
"	2	qr.	Edward Frye
"	"	"	George Chambers
"	"	"	Tar-la-se-na
"	"	"	James Landrum Senr
"	"	"	Ta-ke- Guess
"	"	"	William Bean
"	"	"	Saml Nellums (Two children)
"	"	"	Betsey Cade
"	"	"	George Hughes
"	"	"	Sally Hughes
"	"	"	Yonah or Bear- including Takey- his mother
"	"	"	Cho-es-a-yon-kah Ja^{s} Duck
"	"	"	Inkstand
"	"	"	Water Lizzard
"	"	"	Nancy
"	"	"	Jinny Crittenden
"	"	"	John A. Goddard
"	"	"	Fennel Morgan
"	"	"	John Deerhead..."

Abstract of Payments Made by J. Van Horne Under Treaty of 1835, Cherokee Claims for Commutation of Transportation and Subsistence, Treaty of 1835-36. 1845-55. Special File 154, frame 88, Special Files of the Office of Indian Affairs; National Archives micropublication M574, roll 32.

"Abstract of payments made by J. Van Horne- continued.-

...Year & Quarter...			...To whom paid...				
1838	2	qr.	Lydia Deerhead	"	"	"	John Blossom
"	"	"	Akee Mush	"	"	"	Martin Downing
"	"	"	Oo-le-sut-tee or	"	"	"	Ground Hog Beamer
			Stooping His Mush	"	"	"	Spirit
"	"	"	Jane Beaver	"	"	"	William Tesey
"	"	"	Jane Goddard	"	"	"	Lucinda Reese
"	"	"	Andrew McLaughlin	"	"	"	Susannah
"	"	"	William Holcomb	"	"	"	Richard Radcliff
"	"	"	Mike Murphy	"	"	"	Beaver Tail
"	"	"	Bishop Cumberland	"	"	"	Benjamin Timberlake
"	"	"	Wm P. Davis	"	"	"	Willis Hendrix
"	"	"	John Soon in the	"	"	"	John Wane
			Morning	"	"	"	Squire Tooke
"	"	"	Squl-take	"	"	"	Nancy Timberlake
"	"	"	Caroline Downing	"	"	"	Nelly Smith
"	"	"	Francis Hampton	"	"	"	Owl
"	"	"	John Beamer	"	"	"	Lewis Bark..."

Abstract of Payments Made by J. Van Horn Under Treaty of 1835, Cherokee Claims for Commutation of Transportation and Subsistence, Treaty of 1835-36. 1845-55. Special File 154, frame 89, Special Files of the Office of Indian Affairs; National Archives micropublication M574, roll 32.

"…Abstract of payments made by J. Van Horn- continued-

...Year & Quarter…			…To whom paid…				
1838	2	qr.	Te[?]te-nes-kee	"	"	"	Olly Blackbeard
"	"	"	Dirt Seller	"	"	"	Liddy Blackbeard
"	"	"	Polly Siter	"	"	"	Man Killer
"	"	"	Sally Rabbit	"	"	"	Sarah Doublehead
"	"	"	Tansah	"	"	"	Dick Doublehead
"	"	"	Chicken Snake	"	"	"	Ta-chee-chee
"	"	"	Nancy Timberlake	"	"	"	Cullan I-too-way
"	"	"	Charles Smith	"	"	"	Oo-sow-wee
"	"	"	Buffalo	"	"	"	Lewis Coffee
"	"	"	George Campbell	"	"	"	Thomas Turner[?]
"	"	"	Richard Radcliff Senr.	"	"	"	David Nightkiller
"	"	"	John Cochran	"	"	"	Betsey Downing
"	"	"	Thomas Barns	"	"	"	Mathew Jones
"	"	"	Robert Brown	"	"	"	Archibald Saunders
"	"	"	Tal-las-se-nah	"	"	"	Martin Cul-sow-e
"	"	"	Elizabeth Foreman	"	"	"	Nancy…"

Abstract of Payments Made by J. Van Horn Under Treaty of 1835, Cherokee Claims for Commutation of Transportation and Subsistence, Treaty of 1835-36. 1845-55. Special File 154, frame 90, Special Files of the Office of Indian Affairs; National Archives micropublication M574, roll 32.

"…Abstract of payments made by J. Van Horn- continued-

…Year & Quarter…			…To whom paid…					
1838	2	qr.	Spring Frog	"	"	"	Maria Drowningbear	
"	"	"	Charles M^c^Intosh	"	"	"	Dreadful Water	
"	"	"	Nick-oh-tee	"	"	"	Peter Hog[??]	
"	"	"	Crawfish	"	"	"	Con-ta-kah	
"	"	"	Jack Foreman	"	"	"	Polly Shoeboots	
"	"	"	Katy Rabbit	"	"	"	George Candy	
"	"	"	Susan Chote	"	"	"	Col-lone-us-ky	
"	"	"	Lydia Fields	"	"	"	Robert B. Daniel	
"	"	"	Tuck-a-wall-le	"	"	"	Hawk Baldridge	X
"	"	"	Alice Coffee	"	"	"	Sally Fish	
"	"	"	Thompson Downing	"	"	"	Charlotte Cordery	
"	"	"	Richard Morris	"	"	"	James Cow	
"	"	"	Ben Sinews	"	"	"	James Starr	
"	"	"	Thomas Sooa Killer	"	"	"	Katy M^c^Pherson	
"	"	"	Elizabeth Pettit					
"	"	"	Loony or Redbird	X	wife died at the end of 6 months."			
"	"	"	A-hes-a-tes-ke					

Abstract of Payments Made by J. Van Horn Under Treaty of 1835, Cherokee Claims for Commutation of Transportation and Subsistence, Treaty of 1835-36. 1845-55. Special File 154, frame 91, Special Files of the Office of Indian Affairs; National Archives micropublication M574, roll 32.

"…Abstract of payments made by J. Van Horn- continued.-

...Year & Quarter…			…To whom paid…				
1838	2	qr.	George Waters	"	"	"	Nancy Dryforehead
"	"	"	George Miller	"	"	"	James Deerhead
"	"	"	Andrew Adair	"	"	"	John Culsowee +
"	"	"	Mary Miller	"	"	"	Culsowee
"	"	"	Flemuel Childers	"	"	"	Culsteah
"	"	"	Andrew Saunders	"	"	"	George Chambers
"	"	"	Thompson Sanders	"	"	"	Big nee Jesse- or Jesse
"	"	"	William S. Richardson				Murphy
"	"	"	Lemuel Childers	"	"	"	Edward Frye (X)
"	"	"	Eli Palmer	"	"	"	David Gage
"	"	"	James M^c^Nair	"	"	"	Pheasant
"	"	"	Clement M^c^Nair	"	"	"	Ah-hee-la-tus-kee, or
"	"	"	Robert Still				Dew
"	"	"	Ways-kee	"	"	"	Eliza- or Widow Maw
"	"	"	Charles Timberlake	"	"	"	Echu-ka
"	"	"	George Saunders	"	"	"	Ratting Gourd Waters

"　　"　　"　　Jack Six Killer

(X) added for 1 child for 9 months- born 3 months after removal

\+ 5 for six[?] months- 1- for 3 months- who died 6 months after removal."

Abstract of Payments Made by J.R. Stephenson Under Treaty of 1835, Cherokee Claims for Commutation of Transportation and Subsistence, Treaty of 1835-36. 1845-55. Special File 154, frame 92, Special Files of the Office of Indian Affairs; National Archives micropublication M574, roll 32.

"…Abstract of payments made by J.R. Stephenson- continued.-

...Year & Quarter…			…To whom paid…				
1838	3	qr.	Kattie	"	"	"	Peter
"	"	"	Oos-too	"	"	"	William Beemer
"	"	"	Cah-tais-kee	"	"	"	Cla-na-neeh
"	"	"	Sa, yon, yah	"	"	"	Tes-to-no-see
"	"	"	Wattie	"	"	"	Too-cho-wes
"	"	"	Too-nan-ye-hee	"	"	"	Un-is-ked-ta-hee
"	"	"	Clo-gai-sa	"	"	"	Wall-a-yon-kah
"	"	"	Yah-yoh-kai-la	"	"	"	Kaitee
"	"	"	Robin	"	"	"	Kai-tes-hee
"	"	"	Artsay	"	"	"	Te-a-lese-sa-teth-us-kee
"	"	"	Tai-ka-tah-kah	"	"	"	Cah-sel-lah-wa
"	"	"	Ailsee	"	"	"	Sot-su-cah
"	"	"	Cuy-yah-sah	"	"	"	Clun-twi-tah
"	"	"	Un-tee-all-lah	"	"	"	Jar-kee Wh[?]t[?]
"	"	"	Ah-hil-lah	"	"	"	Jar-see-neh…"

Abstract of Payments Made by J.R. Stephenson Under Treaty of 1835, Cherokee Claims for Commutation of Transportation and Subsistence, Treaty of 1835-36. 1845-55. Special File 154, frame 93, Special Files of the Office of Indian Affairs; National Archives micropublication M574, roll 32.

"…Abstract of payments made by J.R. Stephenson- continued.-

...Year & Quarter…			…To whom paid…				
1838	3d	qr.	Too-sa-wat-tah	"	"	"	Oole-cute-chey
"	"	"	Lyddy	"	"	"	Une-wah-tee
"	"	"	Tis-tee-you-skee	"	"	"	Tee-cun-yes-kee
"	"	"	New-ti-he-tah	"	"	"	Martin North
"	"	"	Ant-seah-tah	"	"	"	Eel-lo-way
"	"	"	Seale-ee-see-thes-ky	"	"	"	Chick-a lu-lu
"	"	"	Taik-ah-talk-ah	"	"	"	Wattee-yan, hee
"	"	"	Wah-sah-tae	"	"	"	Wolf
"	"	"	Tom	"	"	"	End-see
"	"	"	Sianny or John	"	"	"	Ne-wu, you, to
"	"	"	Wah-cool-ah	"	"	"	Uns a lays stah
"	"	"	Ground Squirrel	"	"	"	Chuse-p[?]m-e-tah
"	"	"	John Hammer	"	"	"	Nanci
"	"	"	Che-lu-sut-ee	"	"	"	Cool-aust-tah
"	"	"	A-moo-ka-mars-hee	"	"	"	Scon-tis-hes
"	"	"	Sarah	"	"	"	Art-sah…"

Abstract of Payments Made by J.R. Stephenson Under Treaty of 1835, Cherokee Claims for Commutation of Transportation and Subsistence, Treaty of 1835-36. 1845-55. Special File 154, frame 94, Special Files of the Office of Indian Affairs; National Archives micropublication M574, roll 32.

"…Abstract of payments made by J.R. Stephenson- continued.-

...Year & Quarter…			…To whom paid…				
1838	3d	qr.	Charlotte	"	"	"	Kill-lum,na,yah
"	"	"	Ael-lee	"	"	"	Col-lone-ute-sey
"	"	"	Sia-a tah-wee	"	"	"	Henderson Harris
"	"	"	Jack Conttender	"	"	"	Yau-ne-wall-lah
"	"	"	Che-you-ka-cha-na	"	"	"	Taik-kee
"	"	"	Jack McTier	"	"	"	Coo-tie
"	"	"	Lilly Conishane	"	"	"	Cun tai-kee
"	"	"	Lyddy Harnage	"	"	"	Clunatullsee
"	"	"	Katy North	"	"	"	Ai kee McDaniel
"	"	"	Nancy	"	"	"	Oo-tee-ti-a kee
"	"	"	John North	"	"	"	Oo-sqnal-lai-quah
"	"	"	Sal-tie-hee	"	"	"	Oo-lo-gil-lah
"	"	"	Chu-che-e-che	"	"	"	Che-nan-hey-kee
"	"	"	Kai-tee	"	"	"	Wea. Kee
"	"	"	Ah-qual-lah	"	"	"	Skut-a gus-kee
"	"	"	Tuck-Saw-hee	"	"	"	E saw-kee…"

Abstract of Payments Made by J.R. Stephenson Under Treaty of 1835, Cherokee Claims for Commutation of Transportation and Subsistence, Treaty of 1835-36. 1845-55. Special File 154, frame 95, Special Files of the Office of Indian Affairs; National Archives micropublication M574, roll 32.

"…Abstract of payments made by J.R. Stephenson- continued.-

…Year & Quarter…			…To whom paid…				
1838	3^{d}	qr.	Tom	"	"	"	Susannah
"	"	"	Te-naw-kese-kee	"	"	"	Jim Mankiller
"	"	"	Kel lon-kah	"	"	"	Alexander Smoke
"	"	"	Too-naw-qe-ha	"	"	"	Saw-hicks-atalk-ah
"	"	"	Kate-ugus-key	"	"	"	Oo-ta-hay
"	"	"	Yon-nie-a ta-hee	"	"	"	Conni-cah
"	"	"	Nih-hi-tee-hee	"	"	"	Ska-goah
"	"	"	Cul-lai-kee	"	"	"	San-tai-tai-kee
"	"	"	Oh-cun-nah	"	"	"	Tah-see-cut-tah
"	"	"	Waggon	"	"	"	Oot-see-sa-lah
"	"	"	See-war-tah	"	"	"	Ka-tis-ka
"	"	"	Tuck-a-war-see	"	"	"	Sum-ni-gu-way
"	"	"	Ol-kin-neh	"	"	"	Jack-kee
"	"	"	Ah-nah-kai-kee	"	"	"	Avey- or Davy
"	"	"	Tommee	"	"	"	Jesse Hicks…"
"	"	"	Why-waf-su-tee				

Abstract of Payments Made by J.R. Stephenson Under Treaty of 1835, Cherokee Claims for Commutation of Transportation and Subsistence, Treaty of 1835-36. 1845-55. Special File 154, frame 96, Special Files of the Office of Indian Affairs; National Archives micropublication M574, roll 32.

"…Abstract of payments made by J.R. Stephenson- continued.-

...Year & Quarter…			…To whom paid…
1838	2d	qr.	John A. Wayne
"	"	"	Barney Hughes
"	"	"	Wattee
"	"	"	Jesse Halfbreed
"	"	"	Crying Wolf
"	"	"	Clem Foster- or Tan-char-la-nah
"	"	"	John Duncan +
"	"	"	Nancy Big bear
"	"	"	Tal-lar-se-nee
"	"	"	Corn Tassel
"	"	'	Thomas Starr

+ imigrated [*sic*] in 1834…"

Abstract of Payments Made by J.R. Stephenson Under Treaty of 1835, Cherokee Claims for Commutation of Transportation and Subsistence, Treaty of 1835-36. 1845-55. Special File 154, frame 97, Special Files of the Office of Indian Affairs; National Archives micropublication M574, roll 32.

"…Abstract of payments made by Ja[s][?] R. Stephenson- on account of the transportation and years Subsistence- of Cherokees- under the treaty of 1835.-

…Year & Quarter…				…To whom paid…
1838	2	qr.		Rylee Goddard
"	"	"		Peggy Sanders + *
"	"	"		Nicholas Sanders *
"	"	"	(+)	Rutha May
"	"	"		William S. Rogers
"	"	"		Katy Cade
"	"	"		Neely M^c^Daniel
"	"	"		Joseph Spears
"	"	"		Ground Hog
"	"	"		Isaac Walker
"	"	"		July
"	"	"		Lampson Pryor
"	"	"		Oo-la-nee-tah
"	"	"		John Fish
"	"	"		Nicko Jack
"	"	"		Ty-us-kee
"	"	"		David Timson
"	"	"		Six-Killer
"	"	"		Elizabeth Shoe boots
"	"	"		Crawler Wicked
"	"	"		George Butler
"	"	"		Wallee or Polly
"	"	"		John Toney
"	"	"		Woman Killer
"	"	"		E-yah-cha-kah
"	"	"		Robin
"	"	"		Dragging Canoe
"	"	"		Muskrat

\+ one child- increase since she commuted her transportation.

* for his wife- having married since he commuted his transportation-

(+) self and child- in company with her aunt Mary Ann Harlin…"

Abstract of Payments Made by J.R. Stephenson Under Treaty of 1835, Cherokee Claims for Commutation of Transportation and Subsistence, Treaty of 1835-36. 1845-55. Special File 154, frame 98, Special Files of the Office of Indian Affairs; National Archives micropublication M574, roll 32.

"…Abstract of payments made by J.R. Stephenson continued-

…Year & Quarter…			…To whom paid…
1838	2	qr.	Tee-nah-na-thlah
"	"	"	Nicholus [*sic*] Sanders
"	"	"	Fishing Hawk
"	"	"	Sallee
"	"	"	Richard Sanders
"	"	"	Horn
"	"	"	Bull Frog
"	"	"	Wy-a-lu-ka
"	"	"	Chewee
"	"	"	Su-wa-ka
"	"	"	Peter
"	"	"	Peggy Sanders
"	"	"	M.M- Scrimshaw
"	"	"	Rutha May
"	"	"	Mary Ann Harlin
"	"	"	Dick Boggs
"	"	"	Richard Timberlake
"	"	"	Nancy
"	"	"	Brice Martin
"	"	"	Andrew Ross
"	"	"	Jeremiah Everett
"	"	"	Pheasant
"	"	"	Charles Reese
"	"	"	Jesse Cade
"	"	"	Robert Waters
"	"	"	Johnson
"	"	"	Thomas Boots
"	"	"	William Blythe
"	"	"	Thunder
"	"	"	Polly Downing
			5 Slaves.-…"

Abstract of Payments Made by J.R. Stephenson Under Treaty of 1835, Cherokee Claims for Commutation of Transportation and Subsistence, Treaty of 1835-36. 1845-55. Special File 154, frame 99, Special Files of the Office of Indian Affairs; National Archives micropublication M574, roll 32.

"...Abstract of payments made by J.R. Stephenson continued-

...Year & Quarter...			...To whom paid...				
1838	2	qr.	Aaron Downing	"	"	"	Samuel Terril
"	"	"	Joseph Beck	"	"	"	Sarah Doublehead
"	"	"	Ary Richards	"	"	"	Chu-quel-kah
"	"	"	Ki-u-kah-tes-hee	"	"	"	Betsy Sutton
"	"	"	Ellis Beck	"	"	"	J.M. Davis
"	"	"	Jeffry Beck	"	"	"	Rilee Goddard
"	"	"	Surry Eaton	"	"	"	Thomas Meiss
"	"	"	Andy	"	"	"	Kul-sty-ah
"	"	"	Rachael Purdew	"	"	"	Ca-ta-le-nah
"	"	"	Daniel B. Hopkins	"	"	"	Wah-sah-tee
"	"	"	David Miller	"	"	"	Hiram Landrum
"	"	"	James Langley	"	"	"	Ske-yah
"	"	"	Nancy Spears	"	"	"	Charley
"	"	"	Dick Doublehead	"	"	"	Si. nan. ne.
"	"	"	Chicken Snake	"	"	"	Chi-war-tair-kee..."
"	"	"	Bishop Cumberland				

Abstract of Payments Made by J.R. Stephenson Under Treaty of 1835, Cherokee Claims for Commutation of Transportation and Subsistence, Treaty of 1835-36. 1845-55. Special File 154, frame 100, Special Files of the Office of Indian Affairs; National Archives micropublication M574, roll 32.

“…Abstract of payments made by J.R. Stephenson continued-

...Year & Quarter…			…To whom paid…
1838	3^{d}	qr.	Quatsy
“	“	“	Ah-lah-nal-les
“	“	“	Cuf-quai
“	“	“	Tant-soo-lane-nanh
“	“	“	Sally Harnage
“	“	“	Nait-tee
“	“	“	Wait-tee
“	“	“	John Cochran
“	“	“	Will- or Tes-lese-ky
“	“	“	Jenney
“	“	“	Nancy Downing
“	“	“	William Downing
“	“	“	Wat- McDaniel
“	“	“	Nah-che-yah
“	“	“	Cun-tu-sut-teh
“	“	“	Kis-kunnes- or Jefferson
“	“	“	Chu-kes-chu-na
“	“	“	Te-ti-nus-ky
“	“	“	Hick-kah-nu
“	“	“	Squal-ayon-ka
“	“	“	J.C. Towers
“	“	“	George Hughes
“	“	“	Jacob Seabold
“	“	“	John A. Goddard
“	“	“	David McLaughlin
“	“	“	Ezekiel B. McLaughlin
“	“	“	Charles Landrum
“	“	“	Edmund Duncan
“	“	“	Charles Landrum
“	“	“	Riley Goddard
“	“	“	James B. McLaughlin
“	“	“	Ellis B. Towers…”

Abstract of Payments Made by J.R. Stephenson Under Treaty of 1835, Cherokee Claims for Commutation of Transportation and Subsistence, Treaty of 1835-36. 1845-55. Special File 154, frame 101, Special Files of the Office of Indian Affairs; National Archives micropublication M574, roll 32.

"…Abstract of payments made by J.R. Stephenson- continued,-

...Year & Quarter…			…To whom paid…
1838	3^{d}	qr.	Noah Lillard
"	"	"	Mary Buffington
"	"	"	Big Mush
"	"	"	Jane Goddard
"	"	"	Nick-oh-tee
"	"	"	David Downing
"	"	"	Thompson Downing
"	"	"	John Soon in the Morning
"	"	"	Cut-tanl-too-way
"	"	"	Squire Tooke
"	"	"	Thomas Tumes
"	"	"	Squl-take
"	"	"	Po-sow-wee
"	"	"	Alfred Elledge
"	"	"	Ar-ma-sul-gee

"	"	"	Sie-cul-see
"	"	"	Ca-hu-cah
"	"	"	Wily Butler
"	"	"	William Gremmet
"	"	"	Thomas McCoy
"	"	"	Charles McIntosh
"	"	"	Elizabeth Justice
"	"	"	Inkstand
"	"	"	Water Lizzard
"	"	"	Nancy
"	"	"	John Baldridge
"	"	"	Samuel Martin
"	"	"	Nelly Martin
"	"	"	Culstia
"	"	"	George
"	"	"	Walley McDaniel
"	"	"	Ail-lee…"

Abstract of Payments Made by J.R. Stephenson Under Treaty of 1835, Cherokee Claims for Commutation of Transportation and Subsistence, Treaty of 1835-36. 1845-55. Special File 154, frame 102, Special Files of the Office of Indian Affairs; National Archives micropublication M574, roll 32.

"…Abstract of payments made by J.R. Stephenson- continued,-

...Year & Quarter…			…To whom paid…				
				"	"	"	Jackson Mankiller
				"	"	"	Tesa Guess
1838	3^{d}	qr.	Samuel Martin	"	"	"	Standing Man
"	"	"	Benj. Downing	"	"	"	Jumper
"	"	"	Sitee [*could be Situ*]	"	"	"	Yaw-saw
"	"	"	Cross-Eyes-Watt	"	"	"	James Taylor
"	"	"	Tar-kee-hah or McCoy	"	"	"	John Huss
"	"	"	George Bearmeat	"	"	"	Sarah Doublehead
"	"	"	William McDaniel	"	"	"	William Bean
"	"	"	Richard Morris	"	"	"	Lemuel Welson
"	"	"	David M. Harlin	"	"	"	Elijah Burs[*?*]
"	"	"	Benjamin Sinew	"	"	"	Martin Downing
"	"	"	Moses Fields	"	"	"	E. George
"	"	"	Catherine Vaughte +	"	"	"	Pheasant
"	"	"	Joseph Starr	"	"	"	Tin Cup
"	"	"	Owl				
"	"	"	Lewis Bark	+ Slaves…"			
"	"	"	Watee Murphy				

Abstract of Payments Made by J.R. Stephenson Under Treaty of 1835, Cherokee Claims for Commutation of Transportation and Subsistence, Treaty of 1835-36. 1845-55. Special File 154, frame 103, Special Files of the Office of Indian Affairs; National Archives micropublication M574, roll 32.

"…Abstract of payments made by J.R. Stephenson- continued,-

...Year & Quarter…			…To whom paid…				
1838	3^{d}	qr.	Oo-lu-sut-tee-[?] or	"	"	"	Dragging Canoe
			Stooping Tree-	"	"	"	Robin
"	"	"	Isaac Walker	"	"	"	Woman Killer
"	"	"	Spring Frog	"	"	"	John Toney
"	"	"	Rain Frog	"	"	"	E-yah-shar-kah
"	"	"	Martha C. Mosely	"	"	"	Jack Foreman
"	"	"	Cah-too- or Bread	"	"	"	Six Killer
"	"	"	Anna Seabold	"	"	"	Chewee
"	"	"	Anna Seabold	"	"	"	Tu-nah-na-thlah
"	"	"	Joseph Spears	"	"	"	Nicholas Sanders
"	"	"	Ezekiel Ragsdale	"	"	"	Peter
"	"	"	Pheasant	"	"	"	Peggy Sanders
"	"	"	George Butler	"	"	"	Tsi-ca-hoo
"	"	"	Wallee- or Polly	"	"	"	Tu-wa-ka
"	"	"	George Saunders	"	"	"	Nancy
"	"	"	Thunder	"	"	"	Sallee…"
"	"	"	Buffalo				

Abstract of Payments Made by J.R. Stephenson Under Treaty of 1835, Cherokee Claims for Commutation of Transportation and Subsistence, Treaty of 1835-36. 1845-55. Special File 154, frame 104, Special Files of the Office of Indian Affairs; National Archives micropublication M574, roll 32.

[*Note: this document has been extracted, not transcribed. The information that has not been included in this extract are number of family, transportation amount awarded, subsistence amount awarded, and total amount received. You can acquire this information by viewing the microfilmed copy.*]

"…Abstract of payments made by J.R. Stephenson- continued,-

...Year & Quarter...			...To whom paid...
1838	3d	qr.	**X** Bull Frog
"	"	"	**X** Fishing Hawk
"	"	"	Wy-a-lu-ka
"	"	"	Richard Sanders
"	"	"	Charles McIntosh
"	"	"	Chicken Snake
"	"	"	George Fields +
"	"	"	Nancy
"	"	"	Cul-sant-too-way
"	"	"	Johnson
"	"	"	Dick Boggs
"	"	"	Cah-la-la-nah
"	"	"	Ki-u-ka-tu-ke
"	"	"	Wiley Butler
"	"	"	Aha-sa-ta-ska

"	"	"	Hah-lis-war-take-kee
"	"	"	David Miller
"	"	"	Nancy Spears
"	"	"	James Langley
"	"	"	Te-tes-nus-kes
"	"	"	Oo-lo-nee-tah
"	"	"	Chicken Snake
"	"	"	William Beemer
"	4	qr	William Nicholson
"	"	"	Andrew Ross
"	"	"	George Ross
"	"	"	**X** Raven Jumper
"	"	"	Walter A. Nicholson
"	"	"	Mary Daniel

+ Path Creek, Ala…"

Abstract of Payments Made by J.R. Stephenson Under Treaty of 1835, Cherokee Claims for Commutation of Transportation and Subsistence, Treaty of 1835-36. 1845-55. Special File 154, frame 105, Special Files of the Office of Indian Affairs; National Archives micropublication M574, roll 32.

"…Abstract of payments made by J.R. Stephenson- Continued,-

…Year & Quarter…			…To whom paid…
1838	4	qr.	Yonah or Bear
"	"	"	Cho-u-ayon-kah, or Ja^{s} Duck
"	"	"	Thomas McCoy
"	"	"	Clonu-nah or Lizard
"	"	"	William P. Davis
"	"	"	Cah-sil-lah-wu
"	"	"	Horn
"	"	"	Stand Watie
"	"	"	Crawler Wicked
"	"	"	Wall-a yon-kah
"	"	"	William S. Rogers
"	"	"	Wah-cool-ah
"	"	"	Scon-a tie-he
"	"	"	Nait-tee
"	"	"	Henderson Harris
"	"	"	Anl-seach-lah

"	"	"	A-to-he
"	"	"	July
"	"	"	Tuck-see-wa-nah- or Terrapin Striker
"	"	"	Kill-lum-na-yoh
"	"	"	Cuf-quni[?] or Partridge
"	"	"	Thomas Tumes
"	"	"	Riley Goddard
"	"	"	John A. Goddard
"	"	"	Jane Goddard
"	"	"	William Nicholson
"	"	"	M.M. Scrimshear
"	"	"	Peter
"	"	"	Elizabeth Justice
"	"	"	Aillee
"	"	"	George…"

Abstract of Payments Made by J.R. Stephenson Under Treaty of 1835, Cherokee Claims for Commutation of Transportation and Subsistence, Treaty of 1835-36. 1845-55. Special File 154, frame 106, Special Files of the Office of Indian Affairs; National Archives micropublication M574, roll 32.

"…Abstract of payments made by J.R. Stephenson- Continued,-

…Year & Quarter…			…To whom paid…				
1838	4	qr.	Will-ley	"	"	"	Dick Doublehead
"	"	"	Culstea	"	"	"	Ground Hog Beemer
"	"	"	Andrew Ross	"	"	"	John Beemer
"	"	"	Samuel Terrel	"	"	"	Thomas Meigs
"	"	"	George Fields	"	"	"	Tom
"	"	"	George Ross	"	"	"	Nah-ohe-yah
"	"	"	Jeremiah Everett	"	"	"	George Hughs
"	"	"	Water Lizzard	"	"	"	J.C. Towers
"	"	"	Nancy	"	"	"	Mary Buffington
"	"	"	Inkstand	"	"	"	Ja^s. B. McLaughlin
"	"	"	Brice Martin	"	"	"	Ellis B. Towers
"	"	"	Musk Rat	"	"	"	Noah Lillard
"	"	"	Mr^s. Vaught	"	"	"	Edmund Duncan
"	"	"	Siter	"	"	"	Cah-ta-la-nah
"	"	"	Polly Sites	"	"	"	Jumper
"	"	"	Tuck-a-wall-lee	"	"	"	Raven Jumper…"

Abstract of Payments Made by J.R. Stephenson Under Treaty of 1835, Cherokee Claims for Commutation of Transportation and Subsistence, Treaty of 1835-36. 1845-55. Special File 154, frame 107, Special Files of the Office of Indian Affairs; National Archives micropublication M574, roll 32.

"…Abstract of payments made by J.R. Stephenson- Continued,-

...Year & Quarter…			…To whom paid…				
1838	4	q.	Sally Hughs	"	"	"	Martin North
"	"	"	Benjamin Downing	"	"	"	Benjamin Timberlake
"	"	"	Mike Murphy	"	"	"	Nancy Timberlake
"	"	"	William Holcomb	"	"	"	George Butler
"	"	"	Thompson Downing	"	"	"	Wallee, or Polly
"	"	"	Richard Morris	"	"	"	E yah-chah-kah
"	"	"	Jacob Seabold	"	"	"	Nancee
"	"	"	Charles Reese	"	"	"	Kate-a-gees-kee
"	"	"	John Wane	"	"	"	Tanl-soos-lane-naugh
"	"	"	Rutha May	"	"	"	John Hammer
"	"	"	Mary Ann Harlin	"	"	"	Woman Killer
"	"	"	Eel-lo-way	"	"	"	Ah-chil-lah
"	"	"	Ska-yon-ah	"	"	"	Elizabeth Seabold
"	"	"	Chick-a-lee-lee	"	"	"	Martin Kilowe
"	"	"	Nancy Big Bear	"	"	"	Jackson Mankiller
"	"	"	Walter McDaniel	"	"	"	Caroline Downing…"

Abstract of Payments Made by J.R. Stephenson Under Treaty of 1835, Cherokee Claims for Commutation of Transportation and Subsistence, Treaty of 1835-36. 1845-55. Special File 154, frame 108, Special Files of the Office of Indian Affairs; National Archives micropublication M574, roll 32.

"…Abstract of payments made by J.R. Stephenson- Continued,-

…Year & Quarter…			…To whom paid…				
1838	4	qr.	Spring Frog	"	"	"	Fennel Morgan
"	"	"	Se-wa-nee	"	"	"	Samuel Nellums
"	"	"	Wool-a-loo, or Waggon	"	"	"	David Downing
"	"	"	Martin Downing	"	"	"	Charlotte
"	"	"	Willis Hendricks	"	"	"	Robin
"	"	"	Nelly Smith	"	"	"	Se-yon-yah
"	"	'	Wife of Sanders Chote,	"	"	"	Wattee
			(Susan)	"	"	"	Lewis Bark
"	"	"	Tah-ses-cut-tah	"	"	"	Cun-nie-cah
"	"	"	San-ta-tai-gee	"	"	"	Buffalo
"	"	"	Dragging Canoe	"	"	"	Skeet-a-gus-kee
"	"	"	Thomas Barnes	"	"	"	Lewis Coffee
"	"	"	Lucy Sweetwater	"	"	"	Tes-tee-yon-skee
"	"	"	Ta-lah- or Rain Frog	"	"	"	Cah-too or Bread
"	"	"	Ty-us-kee	"	"	"	A-kee- or Hannah Light
"	"	"	Barney Hughs				Carrier…"
"	"	"	Oo-sow-wee				

Abstract of Payments Made by J.R. Stephenson Under Treaty of 1835, Cherokee Claims for Commutation of Transportation and Subsistence, Treaty of 1835-36. 1845-55. Special File 154, frame 109, Special Files of the Office of Indian Affairs; National Archives micropublication M574, roll 32.

"…Abstract of payments made by J.R. Stephenson- Continued,-

...Year & Quarter…			…To whom paid…				
1838	4	qr.	Mankiller	"	"	"	San-ta-tai-gee
"	"	"	John Fish	"	"	"	Tah see-cut-tah
"	"	"	John Seabold	"	"	"	Wife of Sanders Choat
"	"	"	Thomas Bigby	"	"	"	Walter A. Nicholson
"	"	"	Sot-due-kah	"	"	"	Cun-to-sut-tee
"	"	"	Nancy	"	"	"	Pot-se-sah-tah
"	"	"	Mary Buffington	"	"	"	Richard Ratcliffe +
"	"	"	Jas. B. M[c]Laughlin	"	"	"	Beaver Tail
"	"	"	J.C. Towers	"	"	"	Liddy Blackbeard
"	"	"	Ellis B. Towers	"	"	"	Susannah
"	"	"	Ruth May	"	"	"	Squal-Take
"	"	"	Mary Ann Harlin	"	"	"	Leaf
"	"	"	Caroline Downing	"	"	"	Ground Squirrel
"	"	"	Se-wa-ne	"	"	"	Robert Brown (his child)
"	"	"	Wool-a-loo or Waggon				
"	"	"	Willis Hendricks	+ Jr. on abstract, but not on the voucher…"			
"	"	"	Francis Hampton				

Abstract of Payments Made by J.R. Stephenson Under Treaty of 1835, Cherokee Claims for Commutation of Transportation and Subsistence, Treaty of 1835-36. 1845-55. Special File 154, frame 110, Special Files of the Office of Indian Affairs; National Archives micropublication M574, roll 32.

"…Abstract of payments made by J.R. Stephenson- Continued,-

…Year & Quarter…			…To whom paid…
1838	4	qr.	Betsey Sutton
"	"	"	John Culsow-ee
"	"	"	Ben. Simms
"	"	"	Alfred Elledge
"	"	"	David M. Harlin
"	"	"	Jack Forman
"	"	"	William Pettet
"	"	"	Sally Hughs
"	"	"	John Toney
"	"	"	Tee-na-na-thla
"	"	"	William Beemer
"	"	"	Chick-oo-wee
"	"	"	Peter
"	"	"	See-wa-ka
"	"	"	Wy-a-lu-ka
"	"	"	T[?]-lah-hoo
"	"	"	Wife of Jesse Cade
"	"	"	Nicholas Sanders
"	"	"	David Night Killer
"	"	"	Peggy Sanders
"	"	"	Ary Richards
"	"	"	Polly Downing
"	"	"	Aaron Downing
"	"	"	Richard Sanders
"	"	"	Chewee
"	"	"	Surry Eaton
"	"	"	Fishing Hawk
"	"	"	Nancy
"	"	"	Bull Frog
"	"	"	Sallee
"	"	"	Nancy Daniel…"

Abstract of Payments Made by J.R. Stephenson Under Treaty of 1835, Cherokee Claims for Commutation of Transportation and Subsistence, Treaty of 1835-36. 1845-55. Special File 154, frame 111, Special Files of the Office of Indian Affairs; National Archives micropublication M574, roll 32.

"…Abstract of payments made by J.R. Stephenson- Continued,-

...Year & Quarter…			…To whom paid…
1838	4	qr.	Taik-kee
"	"	"	Pheasant
"	"	"	The Heirs of Robert Berry dec^{d}
"	"	"	Robert B. Daniel
"	"	"	Ruth
"	"	"	Mary Daniel (one slave)
"	"	"	Samuel K. Wear
"	"	"	Mary Daniel
"	"	"	Joshua Buffington (one child)
"	"	"	Samuel Martin
"	"	"	John R. Daniel
"	"	"	Cah-sil-lah-wee
"	"	"	Coo-tie
"	"	"	Horn
"	"	"	Nelly
"	"	"	Art-sah
"	"	"	Thomas Boots
"	"	"	James Kell
"	"	"	Samuel Thomas
"	"	"	Betsey Downing
"	"	"	Oos-qual-lay-quah
"	"	"	Tees a lesse ju-us-kee or Five
"	"	"	Te-te-nus-kee
"	"	"	Mathew Jones
"	"	"	Daniel B. Hopkins
"	"	"	Wally, or William McDaniel
"	"	"	Cun-taik-kee
"	"	"	Cla-nee-nah- or Lizzard
"	"	"	Sea-lee-sa-tas-ky
"	"	"	Edmund Duncan
"	"	"	S gin ny- or John
"	"	"	Ah-qual-lah…"

Abstract of Payments Made by J.R. Stephenson Under Treaty of 1835, Cherokee Claims for Commutation of Transportation and Subsistence, Treaty of 1835-36. 1845-55. Special File 154, frame 112, Special Files of the Office of Indian Affairs; National Archives micropublication M574, roll 32.

"…Abstract of payments made by J.R. Stephenson- Continued,-

…Year & Quarter…			…To whom paid…
1838	4	qr.	Tee-a-lah-hes
"	"	"	Sai-lee- or Sarah
"	"	"	Robin- or Su-win-nah
"	"	"	Sum-ny-gee-way
"	"	"	David Miller- & wife Olly
"	"	"	Ka-tes-ha- or Black Bone
"	"	"	Sal-tee-hee
"	"	"	Te-to[?]-nus-kee
"	"	"	Aul-ly
"	"	"	Young Turkey
"	"	"	Nelly
"	"	"	Sel-ta-ha

"	"	"	Chu-he-sat-tah- or Dion
"	"	"	Oo-tee-to-a-hee
"	"	"	Nancy Graves
"	"	"	Cah-nee-hee
"	"	"	Ne-wee-you-tee- & Endsea
"	"	"	Aikee- M^c^Daniel
"	"	"	Chu-me-key-ku- or Ellis
"	"	"	Jack Conttender
"	"	"	Saul-a-you-ka
"	"	"	Ama-sul-gee
"	"	"	David Timpson
"	"	"	Francis Hampton
"	"	"	M.M. Scrimshear
"	"	"	Richard Blackburn
"	"	"	M.C. Mosely…"

Abstract of Payments Made by J.R. Stephenson Under Treaty of 1835, Cherokee Claims for Commutation of Transportation and Subsistence, Treaty of 1835-36. 1845-55. Special File 154, frame 113, Special Files of the Office of Indian Affairs; National Archives micropublication M574, roll 32.

"…Abstract of payments made by J.R. Stephenson- Continued,-

...Year & Quarter...			…To whom paid…				
1839	1	qr.	Aikee Coffee	"	"	"	George Campbell
"	"	"	Charles Landrum	"	"	"	Bishop Cumberland
"	"	"	Clun-a-tul-see- or	"	"	"	Jesse Cade
			Panther	"	"	"	William Teesey
"	"	"	Oot-se-sa-tah	"	"	"	John Wayne
"	"	‘	Night Killer	"	"	"	Jim Mankiller
"	"	"	Widow Big Dollar	"	"	"	James Hughes
"	"	"	Kaity North	"	"	"	Eldridge Vaughn
"	"	"	John North	"	"	"	James Landrum
"	"	"	Nelly	"	"	"	William Bean
"	"	"	Sar-hee-ka- or McCoy	"	"	"	Thomas Teemer
"	"	"	Sally Harnage	"	"	"	Polly Sites
"	"	"	Oh-tah-mah-lee	"	"	"	Buffalo
"	"	"	John Blossom	"	"	"	Che-quel-kah
"	"	"	Squire Tooke	"	"	"	Se-wa-ne
"	"	"	Martin Kilowe	"	"	"	John M. Davis…"
"	"	"	Man Killer				

Abstract of Payments Made by J.R. Stephenson Under Treaty of 1835, Cherokee Claims for Commutation of Transportation and Subsistence, Treaty of 1835-36. 1845-55. Special File 154, frame 114, Special Files of the Office of Indian Affairs; National Archives micropublication M574, roll 32.

"…Abstract of payments made by J.R. Stephenson- Continued,-

…Year & Quarter…			…To whom paid…				
1839	1	qr.	Charley	"	"	"	Kil-lum-na-yah (or Sam)
"	"	"	Stand on the fence	"	"	"	Nah-che-yah
"	"	"	Jesse Hicks' wife	"	"	"	Ai-way- or Davy
"	"	"	Ool-la-way	"	"	"	Cul-lai-kee- or Chicken
"	"	"	John Kell				Snake
"	"	"	Wah-cool-ah	"	"	"	Ska-yah
"	"	"	Naitee	"	"	"	Che-an-na-yah
"	"	"	Wall-a-yon-kah	"	"	"	James Spencer
"	"	"	Scon-a-tee-hee	"	"	"	Robert Boggs
"	"	"	D.W. Ivey	"	"	"	Wallee- or Polly
"	"	"	Musk Rat	"	"	"	Eliza Drowning Bear
"	"	"	Matthew Jones	"	"	"	Cah-ta-la-nah
"	"	"	Henderson Harris	"	"	"	Jesse Eldridge
"	"	"	Lai-see	"	"	"	William Merrill
"	"	"	Willey	"	"	"	Lazarus Gatlin
"	"	"	Ail-lee	"	"	"	Peter…"
"	"	"	Culs-tia				

Abstract of Payments Made by J.R. Stephenson Under Treaty of 1835, Cherokee Claims for Commutation of Transportation and Subsistence, Treaty of 1835-36. 1845-55. Special File 154, frame 115, Special Files of the Office of Indian Affairs; National Archives micropublication M574, roll 32.

"…Abstract of payments made by J.R. Stephenson- Continued,-

...Year & Quarter...			…To whom paid…
1839	1	qr.	Taik-kee
"	"	"	Ant-scah-tah
"	"	"	William Holcomb
"	"	"	Mike Murphy
"	"	"	Tie-me-ne-gas-kee- or Catches
"	"	"	Thunder
"	"	"	James Langley
"	"	"	Martin Downing
"	"	"	Martin North
"	"	"	William North
"	"	"	Wat McDaniel
"	"	"	Taw-sah
"	"	"	George
"	"	"	See-cat-see
"	"	"	Richard Morris
"	"	"	Woman Killer
"	"	"	Siter
"	"	"	E-yah-cha-kah
"	"	"	O-ma-ut-la
"	"	"	Lemuel Wilson
"	"	"	Elijah Burs +
"	"	"	John Huss
"	"	"	L.L. Bullard
"	"	"	Dragging Canoe
"	"	"	Thomas Barnes
"	"	"	John Beemer
"	"	"	A-ha-sa-tee-ska
"	"	"	Hah-lin-war-tar-kee
"	"	"	Charles Butler
"	"	"	Tee-tee-nus-kee
"	"	"	S. Jenny or ~~of~~ John

+ on abstract- <u>Bean</u>…"

Abstract of Payments Made by J.R. Stephenson Under Treaty of 1835, Cherokee Claims for Commutation of Transportation and Subsistence, Treaty of 1835-36. 1845-55. Special File 154, frame 116, Special Files of the Office of Indian Affairs; National Archives micropublication M574, roll 32.

"…Abstract of payments made by J.R. Stephenson- Continued,-

…Year & Quarter…			…To whom paid…				
1839	1	qr.	Sal-tee-hee	"	"	"	Robin
"	"	"	El-la-way- or Eli	"	"	"	Samuel Terrill
"	"	"	Ground Squirrel	"	"	"	Benjamin Downing
"	"	"	Ar-chil-lee	"	"	"	Leaf +
"	"	"	Big Mush	"	"	"	Ground hog Beamer
"	"	"	Oot-se-sa-tah	"	"	"	Ezekiel Ragsdale
"	"	"	William P. Davis	"	"	"	Thomas Wolf +
"	"	"	Wa-wo-se-tee	"	"	"	Sarah Hicks
"	"	"	Tai-kee	"	"	"	Jeremiah Everett
"	"	"	Quata Murphy	"	"	"	Eldridge Vaughn
"	"	"	Nelly	"	"	"	Charity Waters
"	"	"	Adam Seabold	"	"	"	Jesse Baldridge
"	"	"	Au-ly	"	"	"	Sampson Prior
"	"	"	Tis-tie-yon-kee	"	"	"	Akee
"	"	"	Sinews				
"	"	"	George Butler	+ on abstract- Leap. -}		+	on abst: Stepson-
"	"	"	Charlotte	+ Slaves…"			
"	"	"	Lewis Coffee				

Abstract of Payments Made by J.R. Stephenson Under Treaty of 1835, Cherokee Claims for Commutation of Transportation and Subsistence, Treaty of 1835-36. 1845-55. Special File 154, frame 117, Special Files of the Office of Indian Affairs; National Archives micropublication M574, roll 32.

"...Abstract of payments made by J.R. Stephenson- Continued,-

...Year & Quarter...			...To whom paid...				
1839	1	qr.	William Bean	"	"	"	Tan-ta-tai-gee
"	"	"	Rutha May	"	"	"	Kate-a-gus-kee
"	"	"	+ Nancy Timberlake	"	"	"	~~William~~ Hyram
"	"	"	Robin or Su-win-nah				Landrum
"	"	"	Kai-tee	"	"	"	Peggy Monk
"	"	"	Samuel W. Bell	"	"	"	Nancy Timberlake
"	"	"	James Vaughn	"	"	"	Richard Timberlake
"	"	"	James Fields	"	"	"	Lucinda- Wife of Owl
"	"	"	Dick Boggs				Maple
"	"	"	Benjamin Timberlake	"	"	"	Nait-tee
"	"	"	Tal-lar-se-na	"	"	"	Wall-a-yon-kah
"	"	"	Henderson Harris	"	"	"	Scon-a-tie-her
"	"	"	Sko-yah	"	"	"	Nee-ti-hee-tah
"	"	"	Sum-na-gu-way	"	"	"	Kil-la-co-hah
"	"	"	Edmund Duncan	"	"	"	Kai-tee-hee
"	"	"	Owl				
"	"	"	Lewis Bark	+ on abst. Mary-..."			

Abstract of Payments Made by J.R. Stephenson Under Treaty of 1835, Cherokee Claims for Commutation ofTransportation and Subsistence, Treaty of 1835-36. 1845-55. Special File 154, frame 118, Special Files of the Office of Indian Affairs; National Archives micropublication M574, roll 32.

"…Abstract of payments made by J.R. Stephenson- Continued,-

…Year & Quarter…			…To whom paid…				
1839	1	qr.	Wattee	"	"	"	Dianna Diver
"	"	"	Peter	"	"	"	Liddy
"	"	"	Oh-cun-nah	"	"	"	Ai-lee
"	"	"	Cah-sil-lah-wa	"	"	"	Charly Smith
"	"	"	Horn	"	"	"	Nah-che-yah
"	"	"	Cos-qual-lay-quar	"	"	"	Rider Fields
"	"	"	Jane Conishane	"	"	"	Lewis Griffin
"	"	"	Liley Conishane	"	"	"	John Baldridge
"	"	"	David Cunsena	"	"	"	Robert Brown (child)
"	"	"	Wall-a-loo	"	"	"	Susannah
"	"	"	Jesse Hicks	"	"	"	Richard Ratcliff- Jun[r].
"	"	"	Lettie- or Liddy	"	"	"	Jumper
"	"	"	James V. Taylor	"	"	"	Katy Rabbit
"	"	"	Stand on the fence	"	"	"	Liddy Blackbeard
"	"	"	Joseph Starr	"	"	"	Beaver Tail
"	"	"	Jawl	"	"	"	Olly Blackbeard…"

Abstract of Payments Made by J.R. Stephenson Under Treaty of 1835, Cherokee Claims for Commutation of Transportation and Subsistence, Treaty of 1835-36. 1845-55. Special File 154, frame 119, Special Files of the Office of Indian Affairs; National Archives micropublication M574, roll 32.

"…Abstract of payments made by J.R. Stephenson- Continued,-

...Year & Quarter…			…To whom paid…				
1839	1	qr.	E. George				Head Eater
"	"	"	John Looney	"	"	"	Te-naw-kee-kee
"	"	"	John Drew	"	"	"	Ska-yon-ah
"	"	"	Allen Ratley	"	"	"	Chick-a-lee-lee
"	"	"	Charles Thompson	"	"	"	Taut-son-law-naugh
"	"	"	Loo-cho-au	"	"	"	Cun-nie-cah
"	"	"	Tom	"	"	"	Cuh-tais-kee or Black
"	"	"	Quartsey				Cow
"	"	"	Clo-gar-see- or Field	"	"	"	Chi-kee-nee-nee
"	"	"	William Beamer	"	"	"	Cla-na-nah- (or Lizzard)
"	"	"	Che-wair-tair-kee	"	"	"	Nancy Spear
"	"	"	Ne-we[?]-in-tie	"	"	"	James Kell
"	"	"	Oo-te-ta-sa-see	"	"	"	David Miller
"	"	"	Che-cha-ushee	"	"	"	John Kell
"	"	"	Cher-pon-e-tah	"	"	"	Sallee Bark
"	"	"	A-moo-ka-naw-kee	"	"	"	John McCullough
"	"	"	Skeet-a-gus-kee- or	"	"	"	Lai-see…"

Abstract of Payments Made by J.R. Stephenson Under Treaty of 1835, Cherokee Claims for Commutation of Transportation and Subsistence, Treaty of 1835-36. 1845-55. Special File 154, frame 120, Special Files of the Office of Indian Affairs; National Archives micropublication M574, roll 32.

"…Abstract of payments made by J.R. Stephenson- Continued,-

...Year & Quarter…			…To whom paid…				
1839	1	qr.	Ama-sul-gee	"	"	"	Tai-ka-tal-kah
"	"	"	Cu-he-cah	"	"	"	Jenny
"	"	"	Peter	"	"	"	Cun-to-sut-tee
"	"	"	Wy-a-lu-kah	"	"	"	Che-lu-suttee
"	"	"	Tse-la-hoo	"	"	"	Wah-tie-yon-hee
"	"	"	Se-wa-ka	"	"	"	Clun-tair-tah
"	"	"	Nancy	"	"	"	See-war-tah
"	"	"	Willey	"	"	"	Mrs. Vaught +
"	"	"	Ailsey Eldridge	"	"	"	Cuy-yah-sah
"	"	"	Thompson Downing	"	"	"	Tom
"	"	"	Sam	"	"	"	Sus-sannah- or Susannah
"	"	"	Henry H. Sutton	"	"	"	Tuck-a-wah-see
"	"	"	Nancee	"	"	"	Cool-aust-tah
"	"	"	Cos-tie	"	"	"	A-ka
"	"	"	Yon-nie-a-to-hie				
"	"	"	Nancy	+ slaves…"			
"	"	"	Wah E-yah-, or Wolf				
"	"	"	Ton-saw-wal-tah				

Back East

Abstract of Payments Made by J.R. Stephenson Under Treaty of 1835, Cherokee Claims for Commutation of Transportation and Subsistence, Treaty of 1835-36. 1845-55. Special File 154, frame 121, Special Files of the Office of Indian Affairs; National Archives micropublication M574, roll 32.

"…Abstract of payments made by J.R. Stephenson- Continued,-

…Year & Quarter…			…To whom paid…
1839	1	qr.	Ten-too-woo-see
"	"	"	Tai-ka-tal-ka
"	"	"	Wah-sat-tee
"	"	"	Nee-tah-wee-yah
"	"	"	Ol-kinnee
"	"	"	Un-tie-all-lah
"	"	"	Ailsee
"	"	"	John Toney
"	"	"	Stephen Hilderbrand
"	"	"	Reese Mitchell
"	"	"	Joseph Spears
"	"	"	Richard Drew
"	2	qr.	Thomas Davis
"	"	"	Chic-ko-wee
"	"	"	Richard Drew
"	"	"	Tie-a-la-hey
"	"	"	Tee-nah-nath-la
"	"	"	L.S. Ballard
"	"	"	James C. Price
"	"	"	Mark Tyger
"	"	"	James Lassley
"	"	"	Tee-un-ne-gus-kee or Catches
"	"	"	William Merrill
"	"	"	Musk Rat
"	"	"	Lazarus Gatlin
"	"	"	Richard Sanders
"	"	"	Nicholas Sanders
"	"	"	Peggy Sanders
"	"	"	Sally
"	"	"	Nancy
"	"	"	Bull Frog
"	"	"	Chee-Twee[?]…"

Abstract of Payments Made by J.R. Stephenson Under Treaty of 1835, Cherokee Claims for Commutation of Transportation and Subsistence, Treaty of 1835-36. 1845-55. Special File 154, frame 122 Special Files of the Office of Indian Affairs; National Archives micropublication M574, roll 32.

"...Abstract of payments made by J.R. Stephenson- Continued,-

...Year & Quarter...			...To whom paid...				
1839	2	q.	Fishing Hawk	"	"	"	M.M. Scrimsher
"	"	"	Joseph Beck	"	"	"	Stephen Graves
"	"	"	Jeffry Beck	"	"	"	Kis-cun-nee,or Jefferson
"	"	"	Chu-ma-key-kee- or	"	"	"	Henry Nave
			Ellis	"	"	"	Little Jenny
"	"	"	E saws-kee	"	"	"	Tie-a-lees-ga-tee-us-kee
"	"	"	Jack Crittenden				or Fire
"	"	"	Ant-seah-tah	"	"	"	Squal-Tail
"	"	"	Walley- or Wm	"	"	"	Nancy Downing
			McDaniel	"	"	"	William Downing
"	"	"	Cun-tai-kee	"	"	"	John Hammer
"	"	"	Aikee McDaniel	"	"	"	Une-naw-ta
"	"	"	Cash-nee-kee	"	"	"	Oos-too
"	"	"	Charlotte	"	"	"	Sie-cut-see
"	"	"	Eat-tie-can-nee	"	"	"	James Spencer
"	"	"	Willy Call- or Te-kah-	"	"	"	Che-an-nan-ah
			lese-kee	"	"	"	Chon-a-yon-kah
"	"	"	Un-is-kea-ta-kee	"	"	"	Thomas Davis..."

Abstract of Payments Made by J.R. Stephenson Under Treaty of 1835, Cherokee Claims for Commutation of Transportation and Subsistence, Treaty of 1835-36. 1845-55. Special File 154, frame 123 Special Files of the Office of Indian Affairs; National Archives micropublication M574, roll 32.

"…Abstract of payments made by J.R. Stephenson- Continued,-

…Year & Quarter…			…To whom paid…				
1839	2	q.	D.W. Ivay	"	"	"	John Langley
"	"	"	Taik-kee	"	"	"	Jackson McClure
"	"	"	End-see	"	"	"	Christian Martin
"	"	"	William Blythe Senr	"	"	"	Culstia
"	"	"	James Langley	"	"	"	Aillee
"	"	"	Alfred Garett	"	"	"	Path Killer
"	"	"	Mary Barnhill	"	"	"	Chick-koo-wee
"	"	"	William A. Coleman	"	"	"	John Riley
"	"	"	David Shaw	"	"	"	Aiway- or Davy
"	"	"	John Tidwell	"	"	"	Archibald Sanders
"	"	"	Celia Parris	"	"	"	Andrew J. Miller
"	"	"	Nelly Martin	"	"	"	John Cochran
"	"	"	Benjamin Dougherty	"	"	"	Cull-us-kee or Chicken
"	"	"	Lark L. Langley				Snake
"	"	"	Sarah Sanders	"	"	"	E lo-way- or Eli
"	"	"	John Wicked	"	"	"	Olly…"
"	"	"	Malika Parris				

Abstract of Payments Made by J.R. Stephenson Under Treaty of 1835, Cherokee Claims for Commutation of Transportation and Subsistence, Treaty of 1835-36. 1845-55. Special File 154, frame 124 Special Files of the Office of Indian Affairs; National Archives micropublication M574, roll 32.

"…Abstract of payments made by J.R. Stephenson- Continued,-

…Year & Quarter…			…To whom paid…				
1839	2	q.	Ah-quah-lah	"	"	"	Walter A. Nicholson
"	"	"	Jesse McLain	"	"	"	John A. Davis
"	"	"	Sat-we-cah	"	"	"	John O. Wayne
"	"	"	Oh-tah-mah-lee	"	"	"	George
"	"	"	Jas-kee-Wheeler	"	"	"	Cloud
"	"	"	Richard Drew	"	"	"	John North
"	"	"	Hick-kah-nee	"	"	"	Ou-wa-an-ta
"	"	"	Cul-un-no-ky	"	"	"	Mrs. Catherine Vaughte
"	"	"	Che-yonk-sey	"	"	"	Artsay
"	"	"	John Cochran	"	"	"	Wid-kee
"	"	"	Charles Butler	"	"	"	George Whitefield
"	"	"	James B. McLaughlin	"	"	"	Thomas Wolf (slaves)
"	"	"	J.C. Towers	"	"	"	Charley
"	"	"	Mary Buffington	"	"	"	Charles Duncan
"	"	"	Ah-mush-hair-kee	"	"	"	Sally Harnage…"
"	"	"	Daniel A. Pardue				

Abstract of Payments Made by J.R. Stephenson Under Treaty of 1835, Cherokee Claims for Commutation of Transportation and Subsistence, Treaty of 1835-36. 1845-55. Special File 154, frame 125, Special Files of the Office of Indian Affairs; National Archives micropublication M574, roll 32.

"…Abstract of payments made by J.R. Stephenson- Continued,-

...Year & Quarter…			…To whom paid…				
1839	2	q.	James Martin	"	"	"	William Blythe Junior
"	"	"	Brice Martin	"	"	"	Cah-lah-tah-qui-nah
"	"	"	Joshua Roach	"	"	"	James Lassley
"	"	"	Caleb Starr	"	"	"	Mark Tyger
"	"	"	Mary Ann Harlin	"	"	"	Ground Hog
"	"	"	Etah-ko	"	"	"	Allen Ratley
"	"	"	Orny Utley	"	"	"	John Deerhead
"	"	"	Richard Newland	"	"	"	Con-tai-hee
"	"	"	Kaitee	"	"	"	Jesse Eldridge
"	"	"	Nancy Miller	"	"	"	Aikee
"	"	"	Jenny Pig	"	"	"	Edward Wicked
"	"	"	Ezekiel Byers	"	"	"	Benjamin Downing
"	"	"	Okun-nah	"	3	qr	Che-a-con-us-ka
"	"	"	Chu-tah-lu-ka	"	"	"	Samuel W. Bell
"	"	"	James Mankiller	"	"	"	William Merrill
"	"	"	Nie-a-to-hee	"	"	"	Leaf…"

Abstract of Payments Made by J.R. Stephenson Under Treaty of 1835, Cherokee Claims for Commutation of Transportation and Subsistence, Treaty of 1835-36. 1845-55. Special File 154, frame 126, Special Files of the Office of Indian Affairs; National Archives micropublication M574, roll 32.

"…Abstract of payments made by J.R. Stephenson- Continued,-

…Year & Quarter…			…To whom paid…				
1839	3	qr	D.W. Ivay	"	"	"	Eldridge Vaughn
"	"	"	Kul-ko-los-ky +	"	"	"	John Drew
"	"	"	Darky Bear meat	"	"	"	James C. Price
"	"	"	John M^c^Cullough	"	"	"	So-yon-ka
"	"	"	Scraper	"	"	"	George Whitfield
"	"	"	Jack Forman	"	"	"	Chon-a-yon-ka
"	"	"	Sit-ta-hee	"	"	"	John Riley
"	"	"	Liddy	"	"	"	Nancy Mellon
"	"	"	Dianna Diver	"	"	"	Charlotte
"	"	"	Hawk	"	"	"	Tis-tie-yon-skee
"	"	"	Andy	"	"	"	U-ni-a-lass-stah
"	"	"	Hunter Langley	"	"	"	Betsey
"	"	"	Stephen Hilderbrand	"	"	"	John Catron
"	"	"	Reese Mitchell	"	"	"	Tommee
"	"	"	William Martin				
"	"	"	Dirt Seller	+ over paid- $66 66…"			
"	"	"	Tah-che-chee				

Abstract of Payments Made by J.R. Stephenson Under Treaty of 1835, Cherokee Claims for Commutation of Transportation and Subsistence, Treaty of 1835-36. 1845-55. Special File 154, frame 127, Special Files of the Office of Indian Affairs; National Archives micropublication M574, roll 32.

"...Abstract of payments made by J.R. Stephenson- Continued,-

...Year & Quarter...			...To whom paid...
1839	3	qr	Alexander
"	"	"	Allen Ratley
"	"	"	James McCracken
"	"	"	Omy Utley
"	"	"	Richard Fields
"	"	"	Joseph Cookson
"	"	"	Charles Butler
"	"	"	Sie-a-tah-wee
"	"	"	Andrew J. Miller
"	"	"	Too-na-wee +
"	"	"	Che-a-con-es-ka
"	"	"	James Lassley
"	4th	qr	Omy Utley
"	"	"	Andrew J. Miller

+ or- Too-nah-ye-hee..."

Abstract of Payments Made by P.M. Butler Under Treaty of 1835, Cherokee Claims for Commutation of Transportation and Subsistence, Treaty of 1835-36. 1845-55. Special File 154, frame 128, Special Files of the Office of Indian Affairs; National Archives micropublication M574, roll 32.

"…Abstract of payments made by P.M Butler on account commuted Subsistence- under Cherokee treaty of 1835.

…Year & Quarter…			…To whom paid…					
1845	1	q	A-kee		"	"	"	Path Killer
"	"	"	John Baldridge		"	"	"	Daniel A. Pardew **A**
"	"	"	Sally Bark		"	"	"	Adam Seabold
"	"	"	John Dougherty		"	"	"	Charles Thompson
"	"	"	Charles Duncan					
"	"	"	Ailsey Eldridge		"	"	"	Thomas Wolf **X**
"	"	"	George Fields +					
"	"	"	Willis Fields		"	2	"	Henry Nave
"	"	"	Rebecca Grimmit (+)		"	"	"	Peggy Triplet- (formerly Peggy Coats- wife of Gideon Coats)
"	"	"	Dry head George- or George Justice					
"	"	"	Jay Hicks		"	"	"	Charles Butler
"	"	"	Lucinda Hicks					
"	"	"	James Leaf	+	Including his Brother Jack Fields.			
"	"	"	Jesse Morris					
"	"	"	John McCullough	(+)	Including E-cah-o-sah- & Jenny Downing.			
"	"	"	Jane McPherson					

A	His wife Sallee- children- & Jn° M^c^Pherson- orphan he having been previously Transported by the gov^t^.
X	7 slaves…"

Appendixes

Appendix A

The Cherokee Language and Government Agents

The United States agents who were responsible for the creation of these records wrote Cherokee names phonetically. I have transcribed the names exactly as the government agents originally wrote them down. As a result, there may be several spellings for one individual. For instance, there may be only one entry in the index for '*Culstia*', but there may be other entries for the name under a similar spelling, such as '*Culsteah*'. If you take a few moments to skim through the entire index, it may prove beneficial.

Today, there are two dialects in the Cherokee language, the Western, and the Eastern, also called Kituwah. It may be possible to locate the origin of a Cherokee by the spelling of his or her name. The English name '*John*' is pronounced in the Western dialect as '*Ja-ni*'[8], but in the Eastern dialect it is pronounced as '*Sa-ni*', or '*Zah-nee*'[9]. So if a person is named '*Sa-ni*' it may help to search in records that were generated by the Eastern Cherokee. And don't assume the gender of a Cherokee unless that gender is specifically stated. For example, the English name '*Charlie*' becomes the Western Cherokee '*Ja-li*'[10], and the Eastern Cherokee '*Sa-lee*'. The name '*Sallee*' could be a phonetic version of the English name '*Sally*' for a female, or it could be the Eastern Cherokee dialectical version of '*Charlie*'. Even still, the name could also be translated as '*Persimmon*' from the Western Cherokee word '*Sa-li*'[11]. Although it would be beneficial to be completely fluent in the language, even

---

[8] Prentice Robinson, *Your Name in Cherokee* (Tulsa: Cherokee Language and Culture, 1992), 13.

[9] Marie Junaluska, *Eastern Cherokee Kituwah Language Sampler* (Richardson Texas: Various Indian Peoples Publishing Co., 1994), 9.

[10] Prentice Robinson, *Your Name in Cherokee* (Tulsa: Cherokee Language and Culture, 1992), 8.

[11] Durbin Feeling, *Cherokee-English Dictionary* (Tahlequah. Oklahoma: Heritage Printing, 1975). 151.

just a basic understanding of the Cherokee language would be helpful in searching for a Cherokee ancestor.

Appendix B

Marks, Remarks, and Notations:
Making Sense of Transcriptions and Extracts

When transcribing and extracting the records for this publication, I was obligated to make them as close to the original as possible. However, several items were placed in the transcriptions, but have been annotated to show the reader that they are not a part of the original record. The list below will familiarize you with them.

[ ]	Signifies that the words contained therein are the author's and are not a part of the original or the transcription.
[*sic*]	Informs the reader that although the word preceding it was mispelled or repeated twice, that the mistake was that of the original author and not the transcriber.
[?]	Warns the reader that the transcription of a preceding word or letter is questionable, usually due to smudges, rips in the microfilmed paper, etc.
[*illegible*]	Is used when a word could not be transcribed at all.
Footnotes	Footnotes are used when the author's comments are too long to be reasonably placed in brackets.
[*page begins*]	Notifies readers that a transcribed document is beginning.
[*first page*]	Readers will also see: [*second page*], [*third*

	page], etc. These signify the beginnings of multiple pages. The numbers are determined by the actual pages on the microfilm.
[*end of page*]	Signifies the end of a microfilmed frame.
[*end of document*]	Informs the reader that there are no more pages for that particular document.
Transcription	A transcription is a word for word copy of another document. In a transcription, everything is included: words that have been crossed out, misspelled words, and other marks that were made on the paper.
Extract	An extract is created when only pieces of the document are copied. Just because the record was extracted doesn't mean that the information that was omitted isn't important. Extracted records, like transcriptions, should be used as tools to locate the original document.

Appendix C

Understanding Source Citations

Above each of the transcribed and extracted documents in this book are source citations. These source citations are extremely important because it tells you where you can locate the original document. The figure below will help you to understand how to read the citations used in this book.

The citations in this book always precede the documents that they represent. They are located above the transcriptions and extracts, and are italicized and bolded.

Claim of Eliza Wolf and Betsey Wolf, Cherokee Claims for Commutation of Transportation and Subsistence, Treaty of 1835-36. 1845-1855, Special File 154, frame 39, Special Files of the Office of Indian Affairs; National Archives micropublication M574, roll 32.

"Claim of Eliza Wolf and Betsey Wolf"

This name identifies the document or group of documents.

"Cherokee Claims for Commutation of Transportation and Subsistence, Treaty of 1835-36, 1845-1855"

This is the name of the special file that is located in the Special Files of the Office of Indian Affairs. Each Special File has it's own number and file name that identifies its' contents.

"Special File 154"

This file number helps researchers to identify where to look in order to find a particular group of records.

"frame 39"

On many microfilmed rolls today, you will find numbers located above every page that has been microfilmed. These frame numbers assist researchers by allowing them to pinpoint exactly where on a roll of microfilm a document can be located, thereby saving them time if the document needs to be viewed at a later date.

"Special Files of the Office of Indian Affairs"

This is the name of a series of 85 rolls of microfilm. If you would like to view the microfilm at a later date, you will need to know the name of the series in order to locate it.

"National Archives"

This is the name of the government agency that produced this microfilm roll. Knowing the name of who produced a roll of microfilm is essential in research, because it tells you where to go if you need to purchase or view a copy.

"micropublication M574, roll 32"

'M574' is the series number, and 'roll 32' is the roll number. Knowing both the series and roll numbers are necessary if you are trying locating a particular group of microfilmed records.

Bibliography

Duffield, Lathel F. "Questionable Honor: An Analysis of the 1835 Cherokee Census ("Henderson Roll")". *National Genealogical Society Quarterly* 90 (September 2002): 224-235.

Feeling, Durbin. *Cherokee-English Dictionary*. Talequah, Ok.: Heritage Printing, 1975.

Hill, Edward E. *Guide to Records in the National Archives of the United States Relating to American Indians*. Washington, D.C.: 1981. Reprint, National Archives Trust Fund Board, 2000.

Junaluska, Marie. *Eastern Cherokee Kituwah Language Sampler*. Richardson, Tx.: Various Indian Peoples Publishing Co., 1994.

Mills, Elizabeth Shown. *Evidence! Citation and Analysis for the Family Historian*. 1997. Reprint, Baltimore, Maryland: Genealogical Publishing Co., 2000.

National Archives and Records Service. *Special Files of the Office of Indian Affairs*. Descriptive Pamphlet for M574. Washington, D.C.: National Archives and Records Service, 1971.

Robinson, Prentice. *Your Name in Cherokee*. Tulsa, Ok.: Cherokee Language and Culture. 199?

Suggested Reading

How-To Cherokee Research

Lennon, Rachal Mills. *Tracing Ancestors Among the Five Civilized Tribes: Southeastern Indians Prior to Removal*. Baltimore, Md.: Genealogical Publishing Co., Inc., 2002.

McClure, Tony Mack. *Cherokee Proud: A Guide for Tracing and Honoring Your Cherokee Ancestors*. 2nd edition. Somerville, Tn.: Chunannee Books, 2002.

Language Aids

Feeling, Durbin. *Cherokee-English Dictionary*. Talequah, Ok.: Heritage Printing, 1975.

Holmes, Ruth Bradley and Betty Sharp Smith. *Beginning Cherokee*. 2nd Edition. Norman, Ok.: University of Oklahoma Press, 1997.

Junaluska, Marie. *Eastern Cherokee Kituwah Language Sampler*. Richardson, Tx.: Various Indian Peoples Publishing Co., 1994.

Robinson, Prentice. *Your Name in Cherokee*. Tulsa, Ok.: Cherokee Language and Culture, 1992.

Cherokee Claims

Watson, Larry S. *Abstract of Cherokee Claims Decided by the Fourth Board of Commissioners Under the Treaty of 1835-1836*. Laguna Hills, Ca.: Histree, 1987.

A Few Guides for Locating Other Cherokee Documents

Anderson, William L. and James A. Lewis. *A Guide to Cherokee Documents in Foreign Archives*. Native American Bibliography Series, No. 4. Metuchen, N.J.: Scarecrow Press, 1983.

Hill, Edward E. *Guide to Records in the National Archives of the United States Relating to American Indians*. Washington, D.C.: 1981. Reprint, National Archives Trust Fund Board, 2000.

Kutsche, Paul. *A Guide to Cherokee Documents in the Northeastern United States*. Native American Bibliography Series, No. 7. Metuchen, N.J.: Scarecrow Press, 1986.

National Archives and Records Administration. *American Indians: A Select Catalog of National Archives Microfilm Publications*. Washington, D.C.: National Archives Trust Fund Board, 1998.

Index

The following index includes entries for both people and places. However, it does not include words in which 'Cherokee' is used as part of the name, i.e. Cherokee Nation East, Cherokee Agency, etc. The bulk of the citations accompanying each transcription and extract are also not indexed. but the names of the individuals in the titles of those citations are.

About the Author

Dawn Stricklin specializes in researching Native American genealogies with a special interest in Cherokee who lived in the State of Missouri. She resides with her family in a rural area in Southeast Missouri.

About the Illustrator

Jason Poling is a special education art teacher in the Ozark Mountain Region of Missouri. His work includes murals, portraits, and illustrations. He can be contacted at:

Jason Poling
Rt. 1 Box 90A
Middlebrook. MO 63656